Supportive Supervision in Schools

Recent Titles in
The Greenwood Educators' Reference Collection

Planning in School Administration: A Handbook
Ward Sybouts

School Law for the 1990s: A Handbook
Robert C. O'Reilly and Edward T. Green

Handbook of Academic Advising
Virginia N. Gordon

Handbook for the College and University Career Center
Edwin L. Herr, Jack R. Rayman, and Jeffrey W. Garis

Handbook of Cooperative Learning Methods
Shlomo Sharan, editor

Handbook of College Teaching: Theory and Applications
Keith W. Prichard and R. McLaran Sawyer, editors

The Training and Development of School Principals: A Handbook
Ward Sybouts and Frederick C. Wendel

Multiculturalism in the College Curriculum: A Handbook of Strategies and Resources
for Faculty
Marilyn Lutzker

Where in the World to Learn: A Guide to Library and Information Science for
International Education Advisers
Edward A. Riedinger

Planning and Managing Death Issues in the Schools: A Handbook
Robert L. Deaton and William A. Berkan

Handbook for the College Admissions Profession
Claire C. Swann, senior editor; Stanley E. Henderson, editor

Student Records Management: A Handbook
M. Therese Ruzicka and Beth Lee Weckmueller, editors

SUPPORTIVE SUPERVISION IN SCHOOLS

Raymond C. Garubo and Stanley William Rothstein

The Greenwood Educators' Reference Collection

GREENWOOD PRESS
Westport, Connecticut • London

Library of Congress Cataloging-in-Publication Data

Garubo, Raymond C.
    Supportive supervision in schools / Raymond C. Garubo and Stanley
William Rothstein.
        p.   cm.—(Greenwood educators' reference collection, ISSN
1056–2192)
    Includes bibliographical references (p.   ) and index.
    ISBN 0–313–29652–9 (alk. paper)
    1. School supervision—United States.   2. Educational leadership—
United States.   3. Teacher-principal relationships—United States.
I. Rothstein, Stanley William, 1929–   . II. Title. III. Series.
LB2806.4.G37   1998
371.2'03—DC21   97–21993

British Library Cataloguing in Publication Data is available.

Library of Congress Catalog Card Number: 97–21993
ISBN: 0–313–29652–9
ISSN: 1056–2192

First published in 1998

Greenwood Press, 88 Post Road West, Westport, CT 06881
An imprint of Greenwood Publishing Group, Inc.

Printed in the United States of America

The paper used in this book complies with the
Permanent Paper Standard issued by the National
Information Standards Organization (Z39.48–1984).

10 9 8 7 6 5 4 3 2 1

Here's looking at you, B.K.—wherever you are.

Contents

Supportive
Supervision
in Schools

Introduction

Supportive supervision is a learning situation for both teachers and their supervisors. It often means unlearning old ideas and learning new ways of thinking and doing things. Supervisors have to learn to trust the eyes and ears of teachers, while teachers have to trust that supervisors will use the information gathered to help teachers help themselves. The results will often be seen in more friendly, collegial relations between supervisors and teachers and a better understanding of classroom behavior.

Supervision is thus a method of teaching staff to act in more conscious ways. Its goal is to provide teachers and supervisors with more information and deeper insights into what is happening around them. This increases the options teachers have as they work with students. If the partnership between supervisors and teachers works, teachers learn to identify and resolve their problems, while supervisors get a better idea about what is happening in different classrooms. This provides supervisors with more opportunities to think about their actions and emotions and to adopt conscious plans to improve the learning situation.

Every conference can be seen as an opportunity to provide teachers with the ego support they need. With this support, teachers can talk to children about what is happening in their classrooms. This will help teachers to act more consciously. Action is important; without it supervisors and teachers will not be able to achieve desired outcomes. However, testimonials to the conference process must be taken with a grain of salt unless the process results in more effective teaching and learning by supervisors, teachers, and students. If a supervisor and teacher work well together in conferences, some evidence of improved relations between them, and between teachers and students, should be apparent to observers. For instance, the fears of teachers, or the suspiciousness between them and supervisors, may diminish considerably; teachers may have more self-confidence and satisfaction in their work; students may seem happier in their schoolwork; and children who were formerly failing may be making satisfactory progress.

Consider the case of the reading clinic in a Southern California school district where the students' poor reading skills caused teachers to feel that they were not doing their job well and to blame students alone for their own failure. These attitudes were contributing to the poor relationships that existed in the school and had to be confronted if teachers were to become more effective in their teaching of reading. Through supportive supervision, the director was able to develop a sense of purpose and problem solving in her staff. This was the first outcome of the conferencing system in a supportive environment. As the director became better able to help teachers identify problems, she gave them more power and control over their work in the reading clinic; she saw that teachers had the right and the duty to do their work in their own way. This was an important insight: a pattern of empowering teachers took place, and this was passed on to students. When teacher assertiveness proved to be a success, their rights were broadened, and they became more self-confident. At the same time, teachers were able to criticize their own efforts in the reading center; they began to talk about their own limitations. As they saw themselves becoming more and more responsible for the work, they found it easier to admit that they taught in groups, even though the center was supposed to be an example of the individualized reading approach. This led to further actions, such as learning techniques of individualized reading, that improved the pedagogical efforts of teachers. The effectiveness of the new conferencing system was apparent in the classroom. Teachers and students got along better, and students improved their reading abilities.

SUPPORTIVE SUPERVISION:
A COOPERATIVE UNDERTAKING

Supportive supervision is rarely seen in public schools today. It is a cooperative effort between supervisors and teachers to learn more about what is really happening in classrooms. The problem solving approaches described in this book are not something supervisors do to teachers; they are a mutual effort by the skillful supervisor and teachers to identify and solve classroom and relationship problems together. The teachers accomplish the goals of the supervision team in their classrooms, with the assistance of the supervisor. Supervisors help teachers identify classroom problems, but they do not control how these problems are resolved.

The outcomes of any new method of cooperative supervision are subject to misinterpretations. Teachers may feel good about their work with supervisors, especially when this increases their sense of power and control over their work. But they may not make much progress in their relationships with students. Rather than concentrating on the desired results, some supervisors may focus on the conferences themselves, citing the friendliness and openness of the dialogue. They may note the interest with which the teacher attacked problems and suggested ways of resolving them. Such feelings are better than what we now see in traditional settings, but the final evaluation of the supportive supervision process must be in the management of classroom problems and the empowerment of teachers and students to do their work more effectively.

Teachers must accomplish the tasks that validate their work in the classroom. Supportive supervision conferences may be pleasant at first, or they may be disturbing. If the teacher focuses too much on the feelings caused by the conferences, she may fail to assess the outcomes in her classroom. Supportive supervision can only be said to work when it leads to results that improve the teacher's effectiveness.

The best way of determining whether supportive supervision is helping or not is to insist upon regular mutual evaluation sessions between supervisors and teachers. Both teachers and supervisors can learn of behaviors that are helping the team and those that need to be changed because they are getting in the way. Teachers may believe that they have solved serious relationship problems in their classrooms. This may be misleading, however, because students may be reluctant to speak out about their true feelings. Some teachers may be willing to settle for a solution that makes the problem "go away" without ever really dealing with it. In such cases, the supportive supervisor needs to challenge the teacher to look more deeply into the social and emotional processes that are operating in the classroom. If the supervisory team can get at some of the deeper reasons why the problem occurred in the first place, they may be able to make significant breakthroughs. An intermediate goal is for teachers, supervisors, and parents to be satisfied with the new empowerment processes. The ultimate goal, however, is student satisfaction and improved academic achievement.

THE SKILLFUL SUPERVISOR

Supportive supervision has been shown to work. There is a great deal of evidence, however, that it does not work in certain situations, even when all team members are making an honest effort. This usually occurs because team members are not sufficiently skillful in their communications. Because of the history of inspection-oriented supervision and its hierarchical relationships, many teachers do not see supervision as a way of helping them to teach more effectively. In traditional settings, supervision is not cooperative: it is a way of assessing and recording the perceived strengths and weaknesses supervisors observe in classroom visits. While teachers may derive some assistance from these practices, the record of the past century indicates that traditional supervision may breed dependency and closed communication systems between supervisors and teachers. The authors' research seems to indicate a need for new ways of managing relationships in our schools. Teachers have begun to make their feelings known in these matters, and children are sure to follow their example. Every supervisor needs to understand that new connections between supervisors, teachers, and students are needed to begin the long and arduous process of dealing with the problems of class, race, and culture that so affect the academic and psychological well-being of teachers and students.

When supervisors base on their supervisory and problem solving efforts on the work of researchers, working with teachers can be a continually rewarding experience. A basic problem facing supervisors, teachers, and students in public schools today, however, is not the effectiveness of new approaches, but the poor relations that exist between these three groups. Again and again teachers have been heard to say that administrators are "dishonest," that they speak with "forked tongues," that they are "ineffective," and that they hurt teachers "just to make themselves look good."

To improve the relations between supervisors and teachers requires better staff development and a more realistic analysis of how they see each other and and how they work together in the school building. The disapproving comments of teachers suggest that, while there are many good people in both groups, very few supervisors have the necessary communication and problem solving skills. Supervisors need to become more aware of the mind-set that exists between them and the teachers they serve. There may be much misunderstanding and ill will even if supervisors are trying to empower teachers.

THE PROBLEM OF TRUST

Why is trust so important in achieving the goals of supportive supervision? It allows supervisors, teachers, and students to know one another better. But trust means more than mere knowledge of another person's thoughts and feelings; it implies friendliness and mutual acceptance. Distrust on the other hand, signals unfriendliness and suspiciousness. Lack of trust is very apparent in public schools, where in general, relationships between administrators and teachers are very poor.

Because the new administrator is always an outsider to staff and students in her new school, at first she often encounters suspicion and resentment. Teachers try to figure out her intentions. Will she be able to help them, or will she act as other supervisors have acted in the past? These are some of the questions teachers think about during their first meetings with new administrators. They are similar to questions graduate students ask about their new professors. To reassure teachers, new administrators need skills in feeling, expression, and inquiry. These skills will help them to be more sensitive and responsive to the people they serve and to discover whether the behavior of others is merely an act or a true reflection of inner inclinations and emotions. Teaching roles are played by people who are human beings with names, needs, and motivations. When is their behavior a mask and when is it a true representation of their inner identity? This is the problem of trust (and friendship) as it is encountered in public schools today.

The resistant, antagonistic behavior of teachers provides a starting point for supportive supervision conferences. Since teachers seem to expect the worst from such meetings, the skillful supervisor's first task is to develop better interpersonal relationships and encourage more open communications.

- What can be done to change the suppositions and perceptions of teachers so they can work well together?
- How can supervisors help teachers to begin to focus on their classroom problems?
- What steps must be taken to establish supportive supervision as a process in which teachers and supervisors work together to solve classroom problems?
- How will different communication insights and skills be introduced?
- How can these skills be mastered by busy administrators?
- What will teachers need to learn if they are going to identify and resolve their school problems in significant ways?
- How can ongoing and cumulative feedback be used to evaluate these cooperative efforts?

Recent research indicates that skills in feeling expression are essential if problem solving efforts are to succeed. As teachers and supervisors work together, they go through different stages of development. They establish their own ways of doing things.

The moment a new teacher enters the classroom she starts playing the role of teacher in her own way. As the teacher moves from newcomer to veteran, her control structure, or ego, undergoes a series of changes in response to the problems of school life. Studies of this transitional period show some of the difficulties teachers face. Exactly what will happen to the individual teacher cannot be predicted, but certain changes can be foreseen. Newcomers need and deserve educational support and psychological support for control functions of the ego. They are going through socialization experiences that will fashion them into experienced professionals.

In the beginning, new teachers are transferring their identities from student to professional educator. Children are in the long and arduous process of becoming senior students and young adults. The ego is deeply involved in these socializing experiences. The cognition function needs strong support if it is to perceive and understand the events of classroom life correctly. What can skillful supervisors do to help the teacher's ego perform these important tasks? How can they help teachers to be in contact with their own innermost thoughts and feelings? How can they help them to develop greater sensitivity toward others? And finally, just what do skillful supervisors need to know in order to help teachers function more effectively?

Common sense suggests that supportive supervision works best when supported by the total school climate. Ask different teachers if face-to-face meetings with supervisors are important in solving classroom problems, and their answers may vary because of their different experiences. Talk about such matters with those who have taught in supportive environments, and they'll tell you how important conferences are in solving mutual problems. However, if you look at the practices in traditional schools across America, you will find that very few schools permit teachers and supervisors to talk to each other about what they are doing in classrooms.

Some educators say that teachers and administrators don't have the time to engage in problem-solving conferences. There is some truth to this statement. But if problem solving skills are important, new approaches need to be developed around these traditional practices. Weekly one-on-one and group conferences are needed. The "how-to" of educational problem solving and support takes place in such meetings, where teachers are encouraged to verbalize thoughts and feelings. In addition, in these weekly conferences, the egos of both administrators and teachers are strengthened.

When weekly conferences are held, the classroom can become an important clinical setting where teachers carefully observe, problem-solve, and acquire the necessary teaching skills. Teachers and supervisors use these skills to learn more about what is happening in classrooms. Teachers also become more aware of what is happening in their relations with other teachers and students; their control structures are constantly strengthened as they learn to empathize with others.

Why is it important for a teacher to know how she feels about a student or fellow teacher? Until she becomes aware, she may be unconscious of how people are reacting to her actions. She may be unaware of the double messages she is sending, or the deeper motives for her own attitudes and behavior.

Supervisors are quick to recognize the problems associated with working with teachers in weekly meetings. How can they know what to talk about in their first conferences with teachers? Several methods can be used. At first, a supervisor can listen to the teacher discussing her students and then focus upon those students the teacher chooses to discuss. Another method would be to ask the teacher what she knows about each youngster in her class. The supervisor might ask why the teacher knows so much about Jane and Harry but so little about Juan and Philip. How can she explain knowing so much about some, and so little about other, students in her class? Are the children she knows little about "outsiders"? If so, what is she doing to help them make friends? What is she doing to integrate them into friendship groups? Too often, teachers unknowingly reinforce attitudes of the children in the class. The teacher may not accept "outsiders" because they seem shy and timid, or because they act out to get some attention. Other children are sometimes not as accepting as we would like them to be toward newcomers. They may not play with them at recess when teachers are not around, or they may not eat with them at lunch time. And all too often, teachers who are not sensitive enough fail to understand and support these newcomers adequately.

These ideas may seem very difficult to grasp. A systematic approach to supportive supervision is to break it down into three categories of organization and evaluation.

1. *Information.* Supervisors can use individual and group conferences with teachers to learn more about what is happening in their classrooms. This must happen in stages; however as trust and friendship develop, new and deeper problems will be identified and addressed in the supervisory conferences.
2. *Problem identification and management.* Since the aim of supportive supervision is to place teachers at the center of their own problem identification-resolution cycle, it can be organized around helping methods and Ego Psychological research. For instance, Ego Psychological theory has elaborated a theory of neutralization that can be very helpful in getting teachers to move emotional and impulsive energies into the realm of language, where the ego can exercise its control functions over them.
3. *Ongoing and cumulative feedback.* Since the problem solving efforts of supervisor and teachers are ongoing, evaluation can and should occur every six weeks and, in cumulative fashion, at the end of the year. The supportive supervision method enables supervisors to know how they are doing in their efforts to aid and assist teachers. Using periodic feedback sessions helps the supervisor identify which of her behaviors are helping and which are not.

To return to the crucial initial question: What kind of training will enable supervisors to provide teachers with problem solving abilities? The ultimate question then is, How can these practices be extended to students, who are our ultimate clients? A successful supervisory system will enable teachers to manage their problems more effectively and provide them with many opportunities for deeper insights into their working situations.

Certain knowledge, insights, and understandings will be needed, of course, in addition to skills that can help supervisors through ongoing interactions with others. The blending of theory and practice is essential to the delivery of services to co-professionals and students. Effective supportive supervision requires knowledge of Ego Psychological theory and research, and other personality theories and principles, and a sense of the effects large organizations have on the behavior of teachers and students, and the supervisor's self-understanding.

FEELING EXPRESSION AND INQUIRY SKILLS

Supervisors have to commit themselves to a lifelong learning experience if they are to deliver to teachers (and students) the help they need in identifying and solving their own problems. They will have to gain a greater self-awareness and an ability to use themselves in more conscious ways. Supervisors will have to develop better interpersonal relationships with those they serve, helping them to see that problem solving can only work well in a friendly, trusting school environment. They will have to challenge teachers to see themselves as others see them and to think more deeply about what is happening in classrooms. The only way to learn these insights and skills is to see them in action and practice them again and again until proficiency is achieved. A methodical approach to supportive supervision skills, insights, and knowledge might include the following steps:

1. Learn about human personality theories, with a special emphasis upon Ego Psychology and its use in problem solving efforts and therapy. This text provides an initial introduction to these theories, with examples.
2. Gain an understanding of situational analysis and the structural and relational features that develop.
3. Practice and develop initial skills in training seminars and with friends at home or in school. Here the learner can realize her mistakes and correct them in a nonthreatening environment.
4. Use new conferencing and problem solving skills under the supervision of skillful supervisors. This apprentice experience provides new supervisors with the time to reflect on what they are doing to provide ego support for teachers.
5. Acquire a continual commitment to self-development and learning. Those who commit themselves to supportive supervision must constantly upgrade their skills and insights, using their own experiences and those of others who are working in this field. In interactions with teachers, good supervisors learn that mistakes are normal and that providing support is a process that constantly introduces new variables into the supervisory relationship. Having the necessary knowledge, insights, and skills are not enough, then. Supervisors must learn to use the methods of supportive supervision competently through practice, in apprentice situations, and later in the work place itself.

Each supervisor must make a choice about how she intends to work with people in her school. This book provides a systematic approach for beginners or those with some experience—a practical and theoretical framework for solving problems that develop in classrooms and schools. It describes supportive supervisory methods that lead to actions, actions that help teachers to use themselves more consciously in their work with children. The knowledge, insights, and skills described are not meant to be comprehensive, but they do provide a good beginning for those who want to change the practices and relationships that exist in our schools today.

This book is a handbook for teachers and administrators. It discusses the ''how-to'' of supportive school supervision, and the insights, knowledge, and skills supervisors (and teachers) need as they work in the change-resistant public schools.

1

Leadership Behavior in Schools

QUESTIONS TO THINK ABOUT

1. What are some of the shared definitions of leadership that have come out of post–World War II research?

2. What are the major ways leadership has been defined?

3. Is one form of leadership better than another? If so, explain why. If not, give examples to support your position.

4. What are the organizational pressures on school principals?

5. What are some of the assumptions associated with "theory y" managers? With "theory x" managers?

6. What is the relationship between the leadership style of principals and the expectations of their teachers and classified staff? Give an example from your own experience where a leadership style clashed with the expectations and desires of teachers (or parents).

Robert Brown has just been appointed to an assistant principalship in a nearby junior high school, having received his supervisory license a year earlier. Like most new administrators he is concerned about how well he will do once the school term begins. Brown worked as a teacher in this district and knows something about it, but this school is a new one with new people he does not know. He wants to be a good example for his teachers but isn't sure how to go about it. He has said that he chose administration because he wanted to exert leadership in the schools, but he isn't sure what leadership is or how one uses it on a daily basis.

This profile fits a growing number of men and women who are entering the profession. The fact that Robert Brown is a new appointee who is uncertain about what leadership means is typical of many who have chosen to enter administration after years of teaching.

Like many others, Robert Brown studied leadership at the university. If he reviewed what he learned there, he would be reminded that people have been interested in this subject for many years. However, it is only in our century that social scientists began to study leadership seriously. Before this, research focused upon the traits and abilities of leaders, and how these influenced group members. This line of inquiry was discontinued during World War II because the traits that leaders possessed were also found in their followers. Leadership effectiveness became the central focus of a new behavioral line of research as the nation sought to discover why some officers could lead men effectively while others could not.

In spite of extensive research into leadership behavior, there is still much that is not known about leadership. Major problems in older studies were caused by the difficulty investigators had in separating their ideas about what leadership *should be* from what *consequences* followed from certain leadership behaviors.[1] Investigators were trapped by ideological considerations: What type of leadership was *good*? What type was *bad*? These value judgments made it difficult for them to study leadership variables effectively. More recent investigations have tended to take an empirical view of leadership behavior, assessing it in terms of levels of production, employee morale, rates of absenteeism, and other outcomes.[2]

Robert Brown would find other problems as he reviewed his leadership classes. The definition of the terms "leader" and "leadership" cannot be easily resolved. For many, leadership is an innate genetic characteristic of the individual that cannot be taught in classrooms. For others, it is a part of group processes: leaders, they say, need followers to be effective. Still other writers insist that leaders are persons who perform the leadership act, and that research should be directed toward those who hold such positions in formal organizations. Furthermore, there are still other researchers who define leadership and leaders in terms of their status, standing, and ability to influence others in the organization. In the immediate post-World War II period, there were more than a hundred different definitions of leadership reported in the research literature.[3]

DEFINITIONS OF LEADERSHIP

A good place for Robert Brown to begin his review of the leadership literature would be in the writings of Max Weber. Weber, one of the classical sociologists of the late nineteenth and early twentieth centuries, was interested in the source of the leader's authority over his followers. Why did an individual have the power to decide things, and why did others obey him? Constructing an ideal typology of leadership authority, Weber traced the development of leadership during different periods in human history. His typology consisted of three polar examples: (1) traditional authority, (2) charismatic authority, and (3) legal-rational authority.

Most leadership in the past had been based upon traditions that were passed on from one generation to the next. Rulers and leaders were chosen because of their birth, or because "that was the way things had always been done." For centuries these practices might remain undisturbed and unchanged. Every now and then, however, a leader emerged, whose authority and power over his followers was based upon his charismatic message and personality. While these men lived, there was no problem. They were able to deliver their messages in person and to lead because of their personal charisma. Upon their death, however, their disciples often tried to carry on their work, setting up organizations based on new traditions that glorified the messages of the departed leader.

In modern times, however, a new source of leadership authority has emerged. Men and women are now appointed to leadership positions based upon the requirements and stipulations of laws that are passed by governmental legislatures. The effectiveness of such leaders is less important than their ability to carry out their tasks according to the rules and regulations of large bureaucracies, which have become the organizational form of choice in modern society.[4]

Brown would rediscover that some writers do not think leadership is a separate phenomenon at all. They believe that it cannot be studied apart from the collective processes that all members of the group are sharing. Brown would also discover opposite views, if he looked at other books. Some writers believe that all groups have a leadership role built into them, and that this is part of the natural order of things. According to this line of thought, leadership can be distinguished from followership by simple observation. The individual who can influence others, and who decides most of what is happening is, and should be designated as, the leader.

RESEARCH APPROACHES TO LEADERSHIP: AN OVERVIEW

Robert Brown would also learn that, in the last quarter century, the question of leadership has been studied in many different ways. Yet all of these studies can be organized into four basic approaches: (1) the power-influence approach, (2) the behavioral approach, (3) the trait approach, and (4) the situational approach.[5]

The Power-Influence Approach

Researchers using the power-influence approach have analyzed the leader's effectiveness in terms of his or her power to get things done. How much power does a leader have in a particular situation, and how is it exercised? How important is power in influencing subordinates in complex organizations, and others who are peers or outside the immediate group? Using this approach, some have sought to learn the source of a leader's power, following Weber's ideas. Others have been concerned with the way a leader's personal characteristics and the leadership situation interact to determine how much, or how little, power a leader will have. Another question of interest has been how power is gained initially, and how it can be lost. These approaches have used macro- and micro-level analyses of power to gain a coherent view of leadership effectiveness in groups and in large organizations. More recently, new approaches have sought to bridge the differences between this line of inquiry and those that focus upon the behavior of managers in commercial establishments.

The Behavioral Approach

The behavioral approach focuses upon what leaders and managers do in their daily work. It can be broken down into two categories. The first uses ethnography, observational methods, diaries, and interviews to study the nature of managerial work in organizations or small groups. It also studies the things managers do, and the way they spend their time supervising others. Another interest is in the duties and responsibilities demanded by different managerial situations and the roles, functions, and practices of effective and ineffective executives. Other studies have looked at the behavior of leaders in small group settings and how it influences member satisfaction and performance.

The Trait Approach

The trait approach to leadership studies centers its attention upon the personal characteristics of leaders. The leader's success or failure is linked to qualities of tirelessness, special insights, and persuasive capabilities. This line of inquiry dominated research efforts until 1940, when the United States Army commissioned studies to learn more about leadership in military situations. This line of inquiry has reappeared in managerial research, focusing on leader motivation and skills rather than personality characteristics and mental aptitude.

The Situational Approach

The situational approach uses the situation as the basic unit of research. It asks who the important person is in the situation, the individual without whom the interaction or work cannot begin. It is interested in the type of work performed, the role requirements of members and the leader, and measurements of subordinates' abilities and satisfaction. This line of study also has two basic subgroups. The first considers the behavior of the manager as a primary influence in the way people interact with one another in the work situation. The demands of the group members and the situation itself are studied to see how they constrain or enable the power and authority of leaders. This approach is concerned with whether management tasks are similar in different organizations and at different levels of management. A second approach is concerned with the need for flexibility in leadership situations. The supposition is that different situations will require different forms or styles of leadership. This approach is sometimes called the contingency method of leadership, because the manager's behavior is contingent upon the situation she encounters. These research approaches are described in greater detail in subsequent chapters along with some of the important theories that support them.

A JOB DESCRIPTION OF THE PRINCIPALSHIP

Robert Brown would also learn that, with the triumph of industrialism and urbanism, many schools have grown to enormous size and complexity. The principal's role will depend upon whether she administers a primary or secondary school and whether it is located in an urban or suburban setting. These factors will determine how complex the school organization is, and the type of support she can expect from the community she serves. Nevertheless, the duties of the principal will be the same no matter where she serves or how many teachers and students she directly supervises. This is because the administration of a school has eight basic tasks that never seem to vary. Seven involve the principal's interaction with others inside the school building and the eighth relates to her associations with the outside world. Inside the school, the principal is responsible for (1) professional and classified staffing of organizational positions, (2) instructional leadership and improvement, (3) curriculum development and materials, (4) student services, (5) resource procurement, (6) budgeting, and (7) building utilization and maintenance. Outside the school her responsibilities revolve around her associations and communications with community groups and district administrators.[6]

Robert Brown may remember that the principalship gains its authority from the laws passed by state legislatures and the bureaucracies that are organized to carry out those statutes. Compulsory attendance laws have been in existence since the middle of the last century, and educational systems were established in accordance with them. The principal's authority exists only while she is in the school building and carrying out her legal responsibilities. In this sense, she is a functionary of a bureaucratic organization, and her authority rests on legal-rational sanctions. Yet the principalship position has within it a charismatic quality much like the presidency of the United States. No matter how incompetent the person who occupies the office, teachers and parents will always look to it for leadership. The principal is the essential manager or leader in the formal organization and folklore of the nation. She is the one who must articulate and carry out the responsibilities of the school.[7] The principal is the only legally responsible person in the building and the only person who can delegate authority to staff members. She assesses the skills and abilities of teachers and assigns them to positions. She coordinates the efforts of teachers so that the goals of the school are realized in the most efficient manner. The leadership and management skills of the principal function across the seven important tasks we listed earlier. To do their jobs well, principals must apply good management and leadership skills to (1) curriculum development, (2) instructional leadership and improvement, (3) student services, (4) financial and facility management, and (5) community relations.

ORGANIZATIONAL PRESSURES

Robert Brown would also have to agree with those writers who describe the principalship as a beleaguered office dealing with many of the social problems of modern society. Each day the principal is expected to meet and talk with many groups and individuals, and a good number of these meetings are unscheduled interruptions. Teachers have first claim on her attention, of course, but there are many other individuals clamoring for her time. Parents may make appointments, or they may just drop in when they have some free time. Children may need special services or care. Assistant principals may need advice and consent before taking steps to solve difficult problems. Merchants and others may seek out the principal's attention in order to provide her with services or school materials. Moreover, many of these individuals will have strong opinions about the teachers, or the curriculum, or the disciplinary methods; and the principal will have to listen to their suggestions or complaints, when they have them. Some will be concerned with perceived discriminatory practices against specially challenged children, or females, or minority children. Others will be concerned with what is being taught in science and social studies classes. The only thing that seems to remain constant is the reactive stance of the principal as she tries to do her work and deal with the unscheduled interruptions that often fill her workday.[8]

Mention the word "bureaucracy" to Robert Brown and he will probably make a face. Many Americans don't like bureaucrats and think there must be a better way of doing things. But when Weber wrote about bureaucracy, he saw it as a huge improvement over the way things had been done in the pre-capitalist period. Then administration had been rendered at the whim of noblemen and their agents, and people were never sure which rules and regulations would be applied in particular circumstances. Now administration is performed by trained officials who operate within elaborate rules, regulations, and statutes that seek to treat each individual fairly and equally.

Max Weber enumerated five basic characteristics of bureaucratic organizations: (1) the division of labor within the organization, (2) an impersonal orientation in the way administration was performed, (3) a hierarchy of authority, (4) rules and regulations that governed the way services were supplied, and (5) a career orientation that bound employees to the organization.[9]

If Robert Brown thought about the schools, he might see that they possess many of the characteristics of Weber's ideal bureaucracy.[10]

1. *The division of labor in educational systems is widespread.* Teachers in elementary, middle, and secondary schools have become specialists, increasing their competency and efficiency in many areas. Schools teach scientific disciplines, arts and sciences, and music and mathematics. They have special education programs for children with physical, mental, and learning disabilities, as well as guidance programs and psychological services. Administrative functions have been separated from teaching functions and are performed by a cadre of specially trained and licensed personnel. The finances of the educational system, the curriculum development, the maintenance of plants— all these are done by people who have been appointed to their positions according to the rules and regulations of the school and the laws of the state.

2. *Schools have an impersonal orientation that is both their strength and weakness.* Teachers perform their tasks with a minimum of hatred or passion and seldom get to know their students very well. All youngsters are treated as students and given the same curriculum to master. Of course, the problems of students who come from homes that are poverty-stricken often subvert the ideas of equal opportunity and access to all. Nevertheless, schools try to base their decisions on facts, rules, and regulations whenever they can. They try to treat everyone "in the same way" even though they have not done well in educating children from minority and immigrant groups.[11]

3. *The school organization has a hierarchy of authority that stretches from the teacher, to the principal, to the superintendent, to local boards of education, to state agencies, and legislatures.* Each lower office or position is under the control and supervision of a higher one, much as Weber described it in his writings on bureaucracy. Teachers are usually responsible to assistant principals or principals, who are themselves responsible to those in positions above them. There is a chain of command that facilitates coordination for those who manage these very large educational systems. Nevertheless, this hierarchy and chain of command has distorted communication patterns between teachers who work with children in classrooms and those who are responsible for supervising such services. Principals have found it difficult to get the feedback they need to improve instruction and solve problems before they become too troublesome.

4. *Schools have so many rules and regulations that only a few specialists know what they are at any given moment in time.* Principals who must provide special education children with least restrictive environments, for example, need to be aware of the fact that there are many laws, and that these laws change frequently. Most decisions are not based on the whim of the educator, although certain teacher attitudes do influence the educational experiences children receive.[12]

5. *Employment in educational organizations has a career orientation that binds educators and others to the system.* As time passes, these employees become more proficient at their work and more valuable to the educational system and the schools they serve. Teachers, for example, must attend four-year colleges or universities and major in an academic discipline. They must pass statewide tests or otherwise be licensed by state agencies, and their work assignments are made without their advice and consent. Once employed, they must take graduate credits and show administrators, after a number of years, that they are worthy of being considered for tenure. Teaching and administration are both seen as lifetime careers, and though salaries are poor and advancement difficult, compensation and retirement benefits are usually assured.[13]

ORGANIZATIONAL THEORIES

The work of Douglas McGregor was important in moving organizational theory forward during the 1960s and 1970s. McGregor described the progress of management practice and the improvement in employee "handling" that had accompanied the economic expansion after World War II with some approval. Yet he was quick to point out that this had all been accomplished without changing any of the prevalent theories of management. Most bureaucracies functioned as authoritarian organizations and participative decision making was rare. The originality and potential contributions of line workers such as teachers were ignored, and communication systems usually operated from the top down.

Reviewing his notes once again, Robert Brown would see that the most significant contributions of McGregor's theories were their basic assumptions about human nature. A secondary set of assumptions, based upon social science theory and research, sought to provide organizational leaders with a guide to the management of human resources in modern organizations. These assumptions were organized as "theory y," and suggested ways in which managers could use such insights to improve their performance.

"Theory y" simply refers to a set of assumptions about human nature that some managers use as a guide to their interaction with employees. It is an optimistic point of view that states that people are not naturally opposed to the routines and goals of complex organizations. Their resistant attitudes, when they do appear, are the consequence of their experiences in organizations that are run along authoritarian management styles. The ability to participate in problem assessments and solutions, the readiness to be more open in their communication patterns, and the ability to develop more trusting, supportive relationships is part of every employee's human nature. Management's task is to provide the organizational environment and methods of operation so employees can do their best by participating in the decision making processes of the organization.

"Theory x" refers to an opposite set of assumptions about human nature that lead to very different management attitudes and behaviors in the work place. It is a more pessimistic view of the world, asserting that human beings are naturally lazy and work as little as possible when they are not pushed by management. Their attitudes are irresponsible and they prefer being told what to do. The ability of workers to participate in the decision making processes of the organization are limited by a lack of ambition and an indifference to the needs and goals of the organization. They dislike change and innovation, are gullible and not very intelligent, and are easily taken in by people who do not have their best interests at heart. Management's task is to provide an organizational environment and leadership style that is directive in nature, motivating employees through external rather than intrinsic rewards. Without the active and continuous intervention of management, employees would be passive and without direction in their work. Management is the agency that "gets things done" in the organization while employees must be driven.[14]

Robert Brown will find that the challenge to his principalship is to decide on what type of management style is suitable for the teachers and certified employees of his school. The greater the congruence between the expectations of teachers and the leadership style he adopts, the more satisfied and productive will be his teachers and students.

LEADERSHIP STYLES IN SCHOOLS

Robert Brown would also learn that different leadership approaches have different consequences. Researchers have studied leadership across a continuum of four leadership styles: (1) authoritarian, (2) consultative, (3) consensus, and (4) laissez-faire.

In the *authoritarian approach* the school leader makes decisions without the input of others. He asks for their input and suggestions, but they have little or no influence on his decisions.

In the *consultative approach* the principal asks for staff members' ideas and opinions and then makes his decision after giving their suggestions serious thought.

In the *consensus approach* the school leader is but one of many staff members trying to work out everyday problems and school objectives.

We will not discuss the *laissez-faire approach* since this has been shown in the research literature to be an ineffective method of leadership.

Some investigators differentiated between the consequences of *authoritarian* and *consensus* or *participative* leadership in school settings. Four areas of social behavior were used as a criterion for determining leadership effectiveness in modern organizations and schools. These were (1) *climate*, or psychological soundness of the organizational environment; (2) *data flow*, and its effects on relationship building and open forms of communication; (3) *goal formations*, and the role teachers, students, and parents play in these processes; and (4) *control mechanisms*, and the way in which teachers and students are exposed to the social constraints of the school. Robert Brown would be interested in this type of research because it could help him to understand the typical outcomes he could expect when specific leadership styles were used.[15]

School Climates

Not easily discerned in many schools are the attitudes and feelings of teachers and their influence upon the learning environments of children. *Participative* managing in schools seeks to establish high-trust climates in classrooms, encouraging teachers and students to enter into more friendly, trusting relationships. In this approach, principals trust in the teacher's ability to manage the classroom and to participate in the decision making processes of the school. Administration makes the assumption that everyone in the school is worthy of recognition and respect and that teachers and students can identify and solve

serious problems between them. In contrast, the climate in a school that is man-
aged in an *authoritarian*, or defensive, way is quite different. Relationships are
characterized by fear and distrust between teachers and principals and between
teachers and students. Authoritarian school climates use inspection-dominated
supervisory practices to reinforce notions of status differences in the school,
creating feelings of dependency and distrust in teachers and students.

Data Flow

These management styles also influence the communication patterns of
schools and classrooms. If the principal assumes a participative style, there will
be more two-way communications between teachers and school administrators,
and an openness and spontaneity will be encouraged between teachers and students. Adults and children will be able to integrate their emotional lives into
their educational experiences and will get a chance to become more conscious
of what is happening to them in their classrooms. Consensus decision making
processes will be encouraged, and staff will be able to express their ambiva-
lences and to work them out in face-to-face meetings. Explicit in this approach
is the idea that human beings respond to every situation in ambivalent ways,
and that open communication helps them become more conscious of their attitudes and the ways these attitudes influence classroom work. By contrast, authoritarian management in schools is characterized by a restricted data flow,
which courses from the top down. The use of gimmicks, tactics, and duplicity
are important in this approach, in which principals put themselves into the position of having to persuade staff that their ideas are best. Some typical outcomes
of this type of leadership style are overt or covert resistance by teachers and
students and a distortion of the communications that are sent upward to administration. Teachers, for example, are not willing to provide principals with accurate and honest assessments of their difficulties if they think this information
will be used to punish them in the future.

Goal Formation

Participative management emphasizes problem solving methods that are ongoing in nature. They seek to place the teacher (or student) at the center of her
own problem identification-resolution cycle whenever possible. Principals working in this type of leadership style assume that teachers and students are just as
committed to their education as the principals are, and that everybody will do
their best to achieve their common educational goals. Such principals see teachers and students as individuals who are capable of sustained work over time
and assume that they can take responsibility for what they are doing in classrooms. Again, in contrast, authoritarian managers use persuasion and manipu-
lation to gain the assent of teachers and students. Evaluation is used to provide
extrinsic rewards for certain types of responses rather than as an instrument of

pedagogic improvement in classrooms. Typical consequences of such approaches are apathy and passivity among teachers (and students). Teachers tend to resist the principal's attempts to persuade them and develop subgroup loyalties that can seriously divide the professional staff.

Control Mechanisms

The principal who chooses a participative managing style usually opts for group-selected internal controls. Work is allocated on the basis of consensus and ability, and there are a minimum of external controls. Such administrators usually have frequent conferences with teachers to clarify difficulties and to redefine agreed-upon goals. Open expression of disagreements is encouraged, because this is the only way to get things out in the open where they can be dealt with effectively. Teachers and students are encouraged to develop their own problem solving methods and ways of doing their schoolwork.

In contrast, the authoritarian management style relies upon tight external controls. Teachers and students are inspected to see who is not doing what everyone else is doing. Then these idlers are spoken to and forced to do the work like everyone else. Such supervisory methods create conformity and dependency in teachers and students, further heightening the levels of distrust and fear in the school. One possible outcome is rebellion and a demand for a clear statement of the rules and regulations governing every encounter between principals and teachers.

It is important to end this discussion with some obvious warnings. Participative and authoritarian managing are two polar types of management and are almost never seen in the real world. Often, principals will blend these two methods in their everyday interactions with teachers and students, depending upon the situation they encounter. If a new assistant principal, like Robert Brown, chose a participative managing style in his meetings with teachers, he might be unpleasantly surprised at the results. If the teachers were used to more directive leadership, they might be very dissatisfied with his approach. They might want to know why he is always asking them what they think when he is paid so much money to manage the school. The style of leadership that a principal chooses has to match the expectations and preferences of the teachers he supervises. If they want to be told what to do, that is what he must do in the first meetings with them. When he has developed friendly relations with some of the teachers, he can begin to introduce new ways of doing things if they are agreeable to such changes.

SUMMARY

This chapter focused upon three subjects: (1) definitions of school leadership, (2) organizational pressures and theories, and (3) leadership styles in schools.

1. Leadership has been studied for many years, and most recently the behavioral approach to leadership has gained some currency. This is because it allows for the situation and the different relationships that develop between the leader and his followers. Most research supports the idea that leadership contains two basic elements: task-oriented behavior and process- or people-oriented behavior.

2. Organizational pressures and theories deal with the nature and consequences of the bureaucratic organization of large institutions in modern society. Schools appear to meet the requirements enumerated in Max Weber's ideal bureaucratic typology, yet they differ from other bureaucracies in the larger society.

3. Organizational leadership and management have been influenced by theories that made important assumptions about human nature and then developed strategies for dealing with them. More recently, studies of management have keyed in on important areas of social behavior, seeking to discover the typical results such managerial styles have on the productivity and emotional climates of the work place.

NOTES

1. James V. Spotts, "The Problem of Leadership: A Look at Some Recent Findings of Behavioral Research," in William R. Lassey (ed.), *Leadership and Social Change* (Iowa City: University Associates Press, 1971), pp. 255–272.

2. Ray Marshall and Marc Tucker, *Thinking for a Living: Education and the Wealth of Nations* (New York: Basic Books, 1992), pp. 95–97.

3. Spotts, "The Problem of Leadership," p. 255.

4. Max Weber, *The Theory of Social and Economic Organization* (New York: Free Press, 1966).

5. Gary A. Yukl, *Leadership in Organizations* (Englewood Cliffs, N.J.: Prentice-Hall, 1989), pp. 8–10.

6. Gerald C. Ubben and Larry W. Hughes, *The Principal: Creative Leadership for Effective Schools* (Boston: Allyn and Bacon, 1992), pp. 9–10.

7. Stanley William Rothstein, "Researching the Power Structure: Personalized Power and Institutionalized Charisma in the Principalship," *Interchange: A Journal of Educational Studies*, Vol. 6, No. 2 (1975), pp. 41–48.

8. Thomas J. Sergiovanni and Robert J. Starratt, *Supervision: Human Perspectives* (New York: McGraw-Hill, 1988), pp. 55–60.

9. Max Weber, "Bureaucracy," in Hans Gerth and C. Wright Mills (eds.), *From Max Weber* (New York: Oxford, 1946), pp. 213–214.

10. Sergiovanni and Starratt, *Supervision*.

11. Stanley William Rothstein, *Schooling the Poor: A Social Inquiry into the American Educational Experience* (Westport, Conn.: Bergin & Garvey, 1994), pp. 45–60.

12. Antonia Darder, "How Does the Culture of the Teacher Shape the Classroom Experience of Latino Students? The Unexamined Question in Critical Pedagogy," in Stanley William Rothstein (ed.), *Schooling in Urban America: A Handbook* (Westport, Conn.: Greenwood Press, 1993), pp. 195–222.

13. Sergiovanni and Starratt, *Supervision*, p. 58.

14. Douglas McGregor, "The Human Side of Enterprise," in Warren G. Bennis and Edgar H. Schein (eds.), *Leadership and Motivation: Essays of Douglas McGregor* (Cam-

bridge, Mass.: M.I.T. Press, 1966), pp. 3–6; Douglas McGregor, *The Human Side of Enterprise* (New York: McGraw-Hill, 1960); and Sergiovanni and Starratt, *Supervision*, pp. 164–168.

15. Yukl, *Leadership in Organizations*, pp. 83–87.

2

Leadership in Schools:
An Overview

QUESTIONS TO THINK ABOUT

1. What is leadership?
2. How is the leadership situation different in schools?
3. Why are feeling expression and inquiry skills important for school leaders?
4. What are the organizational pressures on school leaders?
5. What is participative management?

School leadership is a way of influencing others through communication. Yet it took half a century before researchers stopped looking at the "traits" of leaders and began to think about the leadership situation itself. Since then a lot of work has been done on how people become leaders and how they can best influence followers, how they can improve teacher and student morale, and how they can better the performances of staff members and the children they serve. A recent survey of the research agreed on these points:

1. Leadership is not domination or coercion of others but the promotion of efforts to achieve communal goals; and
2. Leadership promotes change but it can also resist change when it feels itself threatened.[1]

Researchers have divided leadership into two essential functions: those that are task-oriented and those that seek to maintain and strengthen the cohesiveness of group or organizational structures.[2]

What are task-oriented actions? Management-dominated leadership theory sought to simplify the organizing elements of human enterprises. McGregor, as noted in Chapter 1, used a "theory x" to designate those manager-leaders who were most concerned with the elements of production. People who worked for them were important because they participated in the work processes of the organization. These manager-leaders sought to control the movements and behavior of their subordinates, forcing them to perform their work in ways that best suited the needs of the corporation. They carried with them certain assumptions about people and their willingness to work without being forced to do so by management-leaders. Management-leadership had to perform certain acts in order to accomplish the goals of the companies they worked for. Since "theory x" assumed that people were indolent and lazy, manager-leaders had to identify real and potential problems for employees so they would not disrupt the work. Since underlings lacked ambition and had to be told what to do, manager-leaders needed to suggest new and better ways of doing things. Because employees were egotistic and unconcerned with the needs of the organizations where they worked, management-leaders had to help them define problems in new ways, organizing their workers into evolving combinations and structures. Since subordinates resisted new ways of doing things, manager-leaders had to force changes upon them. Following the discredited leadership research of the early twentieth century, "theory x" also assumed that workers were less intelligent than managers and easily led into erroneous ideas. Sergiovanni believes that these management-leadership theories have much to say to schools today, even though they were written with competitive private industrial organizations as their focus. He believes that schoolteachers fulfill many of the assumptions of this management-leadership theory, working as little as possible and adopting defensive stances when confronted with attempts to change the school environment.[3]

The information-searching behaviors include asking staff members to clarify their intentions, attitudes, and suggestions. They also include requesting more information or facts about particular operations or problems.

Third, information-giving functions include illustrating points, offering information or bringing facts together, and using one's experience to help staff members understand current difficulties.

Fourth, in opinion-giving, staff members and the leader give their opinions about certain proposals or suggestions.

Elaborating tasks clarify the intentions and communications of people working closely together on projects. Coordinating activities show staff members how different processes or suggestions relate to one another. Some elaborating statements summarize where staff has been, and where they seem to be going. Others lead to feasibility and testing activities, which apply the thoughts and plans of staff members or the leader to real situations, seeking to learn how practical they will be when they are put into action.

There are also evaluating acts, which measure staff decisions or accomplishments against organizational goals and standards.

And finally, there is the diagnostic function, which seeks to point out sources of difficulties, problems that need to be resolved, and the steps that need to be taken to resolve them.[4]

Maintenance tasks include encouraging, praising, and accepting the contributions of staff members. They include providing members with the chance to make contributions and to set procedures and standards. They teach faculty to go along with staff or leadership decisions. Sometimes, they allow members to express their attitudes and the attitudes of the staff in summary form.

Leadership tasks also include evaluating staff decisions and accomplishments and encouraging consensus seeking among staff members. They involve mediating between conflicting factions or individuals, and reducing tensions and negative feelings by using humor or knowledge. This book seeks to make leaders more aware of these maintenance functions by using situations from the world of schoolwork to illustrate points and theories. It seeks to make clear, in plain language, the problems many leaders face in today's competitive, uncertain world. It also provides them with specific skills and insights, which can help them to work well in today's increasingly impersonal workplaces.

No set of instructions can take account of all the variables in the leadership situation. There is no "One-Minute" solution to the problems of leadership in the educational world. Every action of the leader, every way of doing things, is influenced by the relations between the leader and his staff. Every member of the staff has conscious and unconscious attitudes which tend to distort how she sees and understands the messages of others. This can mean that the demands of top leadership are often misunderstood by those they are intended to inspire. And these are only a few of the most obvious difficulties which exist when work is chopped up too much, and employees are separated from one another by physical or social barriers. Finally, there are different personalities, changing problems brought on by external and internal events, and often unforeseen emergencies.

So it is right to ask: What do leaders need to know as they go about their business?

Since they must deal with people all the time, they need some knowledge of human beings and how they react to working in medium-sized or large organizations.[5]

Supervisors must also deal with groups of people, so they should know something about how groups influence their members, and how they can form informal structures which work for or against the formal structures of the organization.

Supervisors must deal with employees who are working with others in complex organizational settings, so they should know about organizational theory and leadership and the ways in which individuals respond to the constraints of complex organizations.

They must help staff members identify and solve their personal and job-related problems, so they should have a knowledge of how to work effectively with different people.

School leaders must often provide instructional support and management for staff members, so they should know something about how this can be done most effectively.

Leadership is also a way of learning about and using information so that leaders and staff members can become more aware and effective in their work and more secure in their psychological well-being. This way of looking at the leadership process emphasizes communication skills.[6]

The way a leader faces a staff member or student can be done skillfully or unskillfully. All educational leaders should be aware of some simple skills.

First, the skilled leader will always try to face the client or staff member directly, showing the other person that they are completely involved with them and their problem. In our culture this says to the other person: I am listening to you, I am available now. Turning sideways lessens the degree of contact and involvement with the other person. Looking away from the other person seems to tell her that you are not really interested in what she is saying. Therefore microskills can be very important.[7]

A second skill follows from the need to show involvement: always adopt an open position or posture when talking to a client or staff member. Crossed legs or arms can be seen by others as defensive postures. They imply a lack of involvement with them and what they are saying. An open position or posture can say to the other person that you are not upset by what she is saying, and that you want to hear more. Of course you could be very involved with the person who is talking and still cross your hands and legs. But the important question is, Am I conveying to this other person how involved I really am? Or am I making it possible for her to misunderstand my attitude because of the way I sit?

In our society, leaning forward toward the other person shows interest and concern for what is being said. When both the leader and the staff member are leaning toward one another, they show their mutual involvement in what is being said. Leaning too far toward the other person can backfire, however. This can violate the personal space of the other person and cause them to draw back and become defensive or frightened. It can be seen as trying to become too intimate too soon.

Steady eye contact is another way of telling a client or staff member that you are with them, that you are sharing their interests and concerns. Conversely, looking away to the side can be seen as a lack of interest and involvement and should be avoided.

Finally, the leader should come to meetings in as relaxed a frame of mind as possible. Appearing at ease tells the other that you are not nervous or preoccupied. If you move about in your seat or seem distracted, the staff member will wonder what is making you so uncomfortable.

Using your body effectively is the first step to being a skilled leader. But of course such skills are simplifications. They won't work unless the leader has developed good relations with teachers and students and listens actively to what others say.

School leaders have to do more than mechanically position themselves when they speak to others. To effectively communicate with teachers and students, they will have to ultimately depend on non-verbal communications and the ability to pay attention to their fellow workers. To sharpen their skills, school leaders can ask themselves certain questions as they meet with clients and staff members: Do I like the person I am talking to? And, if I do, how well am I listening to what she is saying? What am I saying on a non-verbal level, and how is this person responding? Is she taking a defensive position, or is she showing by her body language and presence that she likes and trusts me too? Is either one of us acting as if we are not paying complete attention to the other person? Is either one of us distracted by other concerns? If there are distractions, what am I doing to deal with these problems?

FEELING EXPRESSION SKILLS

Most people, as children, were taught to repress many of their feelings and attitudes. Many come to terms with these feelings, becoming more aware of their own reasons for acting as they do in the school organization. Others do not. The skilled leader can help teachers to listen and respond to students in a meaningful way while performing the same services for teachers and parents.

Few books on school leadership deal with deep psychological problems.[8] The supervisor's purpose should be to understand the ways in which teacher and student attitudes influence the performance of their school work. To do this, supervisors need to know something about human psychology, and especially the psychological theory that supports the "helping method." School leaders need to encourage teachers and students to reflect upon what they are saying and doing in the classroom so that all members of the organization can develop inner controls over their behavior and work habits.

Being a school leader today means changing the old-fashioned communication systems in schools and replacing them with new ways of listening and learning.[9] Since few leaders ever develop these new skills, most leadership experiences in schools are confusing and troublesome.

This chapter, and those that follow, discuss what school leaders need to know if they are to establish better school climates for teachers and students. Just learning these skills will help leaders to work with their staff more effectively, but it will not create good learning environments. That will require still more knowledge, more insights, and more empathy and understanding of individual teachers and students.[10]

Researchers have separated leaders into formal and informal types. The school leader has been designated by the state; she is the legal-rational authority in the school building. But leadership is sometimes assigned to those who can best serve the needs of people at particular times and places. In the classroom or staff lounge, many of the staff who are followers in faculty meetings become informal leaders who create positive or negative feelings in other staff members. This ability of individuals to shift from the role of follower to that of leader is often observed in schools and corporate structures. Because of this, the theory and research into small group life has come to see the leadership role as a shared function, rather than a quality assigned to a particular individual. Nobody can be the "cool and competent" person all the time, yet this is often the front which leaders are asked to present in their everyday dealings with people. Some situations demand personal knowledge about students; others require skills and insights which are most often developed by staff or counselors. Theoretically, the leaders should be those who can do things best for a group or school. But in many schools today, high-level managers are always assigned to leadership roles even when there are others who have greater skills and insights about certain difficulties or problems.

How can leaders be trained to understand group structures and the changing roles of leadership? What must they do to work with informal groups effectively? There are no easy answers to these questions. Yet ways of identifying positive and negative groups and leaders do exist; methods of expressing and neutralizing conscious and subconscious emotions also exist and are important in helping leaders to improve their communications and relations with others. A sound communication system provides the leader with reliable information about what is really happening inside the building. It allows her to make decisions based on a deeper understanding of her staff's personal goals and aspirations.

The wellspring and power of organizational energies are released when people are encouraged to identify and resolve problems that come up in their work. New ways of doing things are accepted more easily when they are the result of participation and consensus. While many preach participative management, few provide strategies and structures that take into account the demands of the organization or the expectations of staff members and children. The process of establishing greater trust and participation, which is discussed in a later chapter, traces leadership from its directive to its more democratic ways of doing things.

How to hear others clearly, how to encourage them to talk freely about themselves and their problems—these are other concerns of this book. Other topics include how to use questioning and group meetings to increase staff involvement and responsibility; how to help staff and students identify and resolve mutual problems in the classroom; how to deal with ineffective solutions and ineffective staff; how to help faculty set goals and standards for their work performances; and how to use mutual and ongoing evaluations to gather information needed for informed, intelligent decisions.

Some of these ideas come from the writer's years as a teacher and school administrator. Others are the common legacy of research which has accumulated over the past few decades. Yet these skills, insights, and understandings are worthless, as many learned leaders have surely discovered to their sorrow, unless they are used in the right context, by leaders who are willing to spend much of their energy on developing better personal relationships with the people around them.

These ways of leading work best when they are part of an organization-wide effort to improve things. But they are also effective when only one person uses them with staff and students. This was the conclusion of research done recently in southern California.[11] The following outcomes were observed by an independent, state evaluator:

People at the school expressed a desire to do their best, even when the work became difficult and they were uncertain about what they should do. Student achievement scores, as measured by standardized tests mandated by the state of California, improved significantly.

Students and staff accepted advice and suggestions from one another and from the director in a friendly manner. They seemed more concerned with the performance of fellow students and staff, and their personal attitudes toward persons in authority improved.

Members of the project became more open in expressing themselves, as they learned to take more responsibility for their own behavior and for the decisions that affected them while they were doing their work.

Everyone noticed that it was becoming easier to make friends. Students commented that staff and paraprofessionals were very helpful.

Everyone expressed the belief that they were more aware of their feelings and behavior as they carried out their work. They were also more sensitive to the attitudes and feelings of others around them.

Staff and students became committed to the reading center and to the method of leadership they were experiencing there. The director used an inquiry method, and her own good personal relations with her staff, to communicate in a more open, meaningful way.

Both staff and students expressed willingness to try new ways of doing things once the new situation was understood and accepted by them. Mistakes were more easily accepted as occasions during which new learning could occur.

The levels of responsibility and inner controls of behavior increased significantly and were reflected in the higher achievement and cooperative attitudes of members.

Supportive feedback was provided for every person in the project through the establishment of ongoing individual and group conferences. The director evaluated her staff in individual meetings, and this process was a mutual one which included staff evaluations of the director's ability to help them.

These findings surprised the state evaluator, who was impressed with the positive attitudes and behavior of staff and students working together in this public school.

From this study, we can draw some conclusions about successful school leadership. It begins with the needs and concerns of people and proceeds, over time, to new levels of trust, involvement, and understanding. It is flexible. The methods leaders employ to minimize staff anxiety vary with each individual staff member and student. This is a common sense approach good leaders have used for years. Yet adopting this flexible style has not been adequately debated, especially as it relates to our tradition-bound schools.

Summing up, the this section on school leadership focuses on what is really happening inside the school or classroom.[12] In a later chapter on new forms of administration, the introduction of democratic values is suggested as a goal. To accomplish this, certain key changes need to be made. Teachers must be drawn out of their cellular isolation in classrooms; they must be organized so that they have the time and energy to participate in administrative decision making processes; and these acts of empowerment need to be broadened to include community members and parents.

No one who has studied the schools can fail to see that a triumph of technology has begun to occur—a triumph which demands ever higher levels of efficiency and production. In businesses and schools today a revolution in computer-based and robotic machines is taking place as our society creates mass institutions to deal with the huge populations in American and world society. School leaders are learning that there is a human cost which must be paid: work becomes more and more routinized and mechanical; millions are being laid off and forced to learn new skills and competencies. Everyone wants to be treated as a competent and worthwhile person, as someone who is more than a cog in the machine of an organizational system. People are becoming less satisfied with the work they are being asked to do on the job and in the schools. They want to have more power to decide how they do their work. They want their work to be more meaningful, and they want to end the feelings of social isolation many feel as they work next to hundreds and thousands of unknown others.[13]

This section seeks to provide leaders with new ways of communicating with the people they serve. If school administrators want to use the authority of their offices effectively, they will move away from directive forms of coercion because, in the long run, these are the least efficient ways of doing things. If they want to have greater participation and involvement, they will have to learn more about the way teachers and students think and feel about what is happening to them in their schools. If they want to know what is really happening, they will have to learn about Ego Psychology and inquiry methods which can help them to establish supportive environments in their buildings.

Finally, this section on leadership behavior in schools deals with organizational and instructional leadership. It does not and cannot predict what will happen once these new communication systems are in place. There are many ways to do teaching and supervisory work. The results will vary, as the people in our schools differ from one another across this country. What school leaders can be sure about, however, is that these new ways of doing things will involve everyone in a communication and problem solving process which allows them to become more aware and more committed to their schoolwork. Morale will improve and learning will increase as teachers, students, and parents make themselves heard and understood.

This new way of organizing our schools will also help teachers improve their relations with each other. It will allow them to work out better ways of doing their work. It will help leaders improve their communication with teachers so that pedagogical mistakes are avoided or limited when they do occur. It will help them and their teachers deal more intelligently with the problems and concerns of those being served by the school. In addition it will help teachers and students assume more responsibility for their behavior and schoolwork in the classroom situation.

These outcomes are possible once the school leader learns the basic interpersonal, communication, problem solving, and supervisory skills associated with good learning environments. As supervisors begin to provide a work environment in which teachers (and students) can find greater relevance and meaning in their school work, they will reap the benefits of increased involvement and participation. When leaders open the lines of communication, they learn things that help them to act in more intelligent, humane ways. This makes them more effective persons who make more informed decisions.

LEADERSHIP BEHAVIOR MODELS

Becoming a school administrator puts the new leader in the limelight. After her appointment, she may have trouble balancing the needs of teachers with those of bureaucrats who are in higher positions of authority in the school organization. She may find that people are acting differently toward her than when she was a teacher. Almost certainly she will come into contact with individuals who question her ability and ways of doing things. Some of these individuals will show their feelings openly; others will save their most severe comments for the privacy of restrooms.

Moreover, the new school administrator will discover that some teachers want to be told what to do and how to do it, while others need more freedom to perform their work as they see fit. Some old-timers may like it best if she rarely bothers them. Others may wonder whether she can help them to do their work more efficiently or whether she will hurt them in some way. The new administrator has to accept the possibility that it will take some time before teachers forget their stereotypes of school administrators and come to see her as she really is.[14]

Becoming the school leader brings the new supervisor's behavior into sharper focus. Teachers, parents, and students will see her as either a bossy, directive manager or a people-centered, problem-solving facilitator. She will either use her authority to decide and ''sell'' others on her plans or use group processes to provide more participation and freedom for her teaching staff.

Even if the new administrator is a permissive leader, she should be prepared for this approach to fail in many instances. Sometimes teachers want and expect her to lead, to show them the way. "That's what she gets paid for!" they will say among themselves. Sometimes her access to new information and her deeper commitment to the work at hand may push her into more directive forms of leadership. This is all right as long as she talks to her teachers and helps them to see why she acted as she did in a particular situation.

People have their own ways of responding to persons in positions of authority. Often, they think back to how they dealt with such persons in the past. As children, they learned to protect themselves from the powerful adults who ruled their lives. Every school leader has to deal with the old attitudes people carry around with them. These attitudes create rigidities in the symbolic perceptions that characterize relationships between individuals in the school organization; they create distortions and anxiety in teachers, parents, and students. Anxiety, as Harry Stack Sullivan has taught us, is an important element governing distortions that occur in human perceptions and relationships. People and places that provoke teachers or evoke their anxiety will often be seen by them in ways that are distorted and misunderstood.[15] Ideas and images from an individual's past may interfere with her ability to respond to the realities of ongoing situations. The teacher's responses will often be governed by these old images rather than by current behavior. Every time a school leader directs, she generates attitudes that may be rooted in other older experiences. Her teaching staff may think back to earlier times when they were continually told what to do and how to do it, and they may respond to persons in authority in unconscious ways. Administrators who want to be more effective leaders will have to learn how to free themselves and their teachers from the distortions these compulsive attitudes create in the school setting.

These impulsive ways of responding to authority also come into play when a school leader tries to persuade others to accept a decision she has made unilaterally. The teachers receive some recognition in this sort of exchange, but few people like to be manipulated in this way. The self-esteem of teachers usually organizes itself so as to hide the unpleasant feelings generated by such leadership behaviors, either by confining them to private expressions at home or eliminating them entirely from their consciousness. Teachers who cope with these situations through repression tend to present an image of passive acceptance. Nevertheless, it is better for a school administrator to try to make others understand and support her decisions than to unilaterally make decisions and ignore the feelings (and competencies) of others.[16]

When an individual is placed as an administrator in a school, she may present her ideas to teachers and then ask for comments or questions. This permits teachers to get a better idea of the thinking that went into her decisions. Their insights are enhanced as they learn what she is trying to accomplish in the organization. This "give and take" helps the school leader to learn about the teachers' concerns and the potential pitfalls of her new ideas.

If teachers are not included in the development of decisions, they often respond to them negatively, even when the decisions could make things better for them. Old defensive strategies are evoked, defenses that may have been appropriate during earlier periods in their lives but are now merely distortions and liabilities.

Some leaders choose to present their teachers with decisions that can be changed after a group discussion. This allows staff members to influence decisions, but the initiative for identifying problems and suggesting needed changes remains with the administration.

Some school leaders present problems to their teachers and then ask for suggestions before making their final decisions. Some define the limits within which teachers can make decisions about their working conditions. Other leaders may only permit teachers to make decisions that affect their relationships with students.

These types of leadership behavior represent a continuum from boss-centered leadership to subordinate-centered leadership. It may be tempting to label some of these behaviors as good or bad. However, all of these behaviors tend to generate much anxiety if they are not preceded by the construction of good personal relationships between administrators and teachers; and all of them can be effective in the right circumstance, with the right group, and in pursuit of common goals.

Scale I Continuum of Leadership Actions[17]

School leader

1. makes decision and announces it.

2. ''sells'' decision.

3. presents ideas and invites questions.

4. presents tentative decision, subject to change.

5. presents problems, gets suggestions, makes decisions.

6. defines limits; asks subordinates to make decision.

7. permits subordinates to function within limits defined by her.

Directive leadership tends to create high levels of anxiety and dependency in staff members. The school leader tells teachers what they are going to do, how they are going to do it, and with whom they are going to do it. Staff members are placed in the position of children: they are always looking toward the administrator for approval and direction.

Therefore this type of leadership establishes communication problems in school organizations. Administrators are supposed to make intelligent decisions about pedagogical matters and staff morale. Yet they behave in ways that often prevent them from learning what is actually happening in the enclosed classrooms that characterize so many schools today. Even when they do ask for feedback from teachers, the information is often colored by what teachers think they ought to say. In the eyes of the staff member, the administrator may be an outsider who shares the dominant assumptions of district-wide administrators.[18] These assumptions are not secret. They include the idea that teachers are disinterested, apathetic individuals who make unnecessary mistakes and create duplication and waste in the organization. They are seldom loyal to the school district that employs them and are only interested in making more money and teaching fewer students and classes.[19]

Argyris has pointed out the formidable problems associated with this type of managerial approach. A school leader is seen as the authority person in the building. To gain the respect of teachers, parents, and students, new administrators need to possess important skills in interpersonal relations, communication, problem solving, and staff supervision. Only then can they gain the information they need to function effectively. Only in this way can they provide teachers with mechanisms that increase staff involvement and participation in the increasingly complex school organizations of today.

"Those who can, do; those who can't, teach!" is still heard in many places. Some school leaders seem to believe this old canard, even though it is not supported by research. In the past, when business organizations were smaller and there was less political pressure, it was possible for school leaders to think only about what they wanted to accomplish, how they saw things, and how they felt about the progress and productivity of their unit or agency. As organizations became more complex, many leaders realized they would have to change their way of doing things; they would have to seek more than order and cost-efficiency; they would have to become more employee-centered in their leadership actions. The interests, concerns, and attitudes of staff were important because employees did the actual work and knew firsthand about the problems they encountered on the production line or in the enclosed classrooms of modern schools.

CHOOSING A LEADERSHIP STYLE

Before deciding what leadership style to adopt in their school, all new administrators need to think about three things: themselves, their professional and support staff, and the situation within which their leadership will occur.

The school leader's behavior is an expression of her unique personality. When she assumes the position of school administrator, ideas and values that were fashioned during earlier times are brought into question. Should teachers be given an opportunity to share in the problem solving and decision making in the organization? If so, how much of a share should they have? Perhaps the school leader has come to believe that, since she is paid to be the responsible person, she should decide things inside the building. Should teacher productivity and accountability be her first concern? Or should the morale and well-being of teachers and students also be considered?

Another idea a new administrator may carry into her new situation is that teachers can only "share ignorance" when they work together to solve problems. After all, she may think, she is the one who has worked overtime to gain knowledge and insight into educational matters. She is the one best qualified to solve pedagogical and administrative problems.

Obviously, many new administrators do not accept these types of attitudes or values. They believe administrators can be less directive and more a team leader rather than a "boss." With patience, understanding, and courage to do things differently, leaders will stand up to the conventional wisdom and cynicism of some parents and educators. The school leader who allows her staff to decide matters gives up some control. If she does this, she cannot be sure of the outcome and may find herself uncomfortable trying out new ideas she doesn't have much confidence in. She has to be willing to try out new approaches and make some mistakes if the new approaches to administration are to work.

Of course the new administrator should not choose a leadership style without first talking to teachers, and without taking a long, hard look at her own goals and aspirations. Each school administrator possesses a distinct personality and way of doing things. Each has a set of expectations about themselves and how they should behave as the school leader. Therefore, before taking over her official duties, a school leader should talk to some of the teachers and parents she will be working with. What kind of leadership have they experienced in the past? How did they respond to it? Is there another way they might prefer to be dealt with? Some of them may need greater autonomy and freedom to do their jobs well, others may not. As new administrators, leaders ought to begin by giving teachers, as much as possible, the direction or autonomy they desire. The following are some of the other considerations the school administrator should attend to as she prepares to assume her new duties.

1. How important is it for teachers to have clear-cut, simple work directives from their administrator?

2. How interested are teachers in participating in the identification and resolution of work-related problems in their classrooms and in the school?

3. How well do teachers understand the goals of the school organization? How committed are they to attaining those goals?

4. Do teachers have the knowledge, insights, and skills to work on the problems they identify?

5. How willing are teachers to accept less authoritarian, less directive styles of leadership? Some teachers are anxious when asked to participate in the organizational life of the school. But others, who have had experience with such leadership styles, may balk at the school leader who tries to tell them how to do their work in the classroom.[20]

It follows, then, that a school leader becomes more effective when she meets the expectations of teachers, at least in their first encounters. Later, after better relations have been established, the process of moving from directive to more democratic forms of leadership can begin. The following chapters of this book discuss the observational and inquiry skills that are needed to make the transition from less personal to more personal work environments, from anxiety-provoking to more trusting communication patterns inside the school organization.[21] No longer is it necessary to witness the apathy and decreasing involvement of many teachers. Through the use of sociometric analysis, administrators can identify leaders and followers on their professional staff; they can learn to deal with informal leaders in ways that help the organization achieve its stated goals.

HUMAN DEVELOPMENT AND SCHOOLS

Using a psychological approach to leadership in schools does not tell us enough about the nature of schooling in modern society. The problems associated with educating youth are pretty much accepted by most researchers.[22]

In today's world, people are often dissatisfied with the work they do in large organizations. If they didn't need the money, many of them wouldn't work in the factories, offices, and urban schools of our nation. Perhaps this is because they have so little power, so little say in deciding things in the workplace. If they fail to act properly, they may suffer punishment or dismissal. If they fail to concentrate on the meaningless, segmented work, if they become bored, if they become turned off by pedagogical approaches that are not working for them, they may experience feelings of anxiety and alienation. Even when leaders explain to staff members why schoolwork has to be so fact-oriented, they soon find that teachers (and workers in factories and offices) are unable to put their best efforts into their work.

The reason for this is well-known and generally accepted by social psychologists.[23] Individuals grow from a passive, dependent state as infants to ever increasing levels of activity and self-assertiveness. There is a continuous movement toward greater self-determination and initiative as adolescents grow into young men and women. However, modern organizations often ask their employees to behave in unassertive, dependent ways in order to mesh their actions with those of others around them.

One of the important needs of educators is to find relationships that are more meaningful to them and to the children they serve. True, the depersonalized environments of modern organizational life make this difficult to accomplish. But a school leader's success will often be measured, in part, by her ability to free teachers from the casual, erratic associations that exist in many public schools today.

Administrators, then, are caught in the middle, like most middle managers in corporate society. They have to meet the demands of their superiors for greater accountability and efficiency while also trying to serve the needs of their teaching staff and students. They have to supervise teachers who sometimes feel dependent, passive, and apathetic about their work. At the same time, they have to show those in higher authority in the organization that their supervisory methods are increasing student achievement levels. This push toward greater achievement can conflict with the school leader's desire to change the mechanistic nature of schoolwork, which is often geared to the standardized tests that drive many accountability systems today.

An effective school leader has to find ways of involving her staff in the planning and execution of their work so it becomes more meaningful to them and to the students they are working with. Simple, standardized curriculums need to be replaced by new pedagogies that emphasize inquiry methods and creative thinking. Even more important, the school leader needs to find ways of giving teachers more power and responsibility over the tasks they perform in the school organization. She needs to learn how to resolve interpersonal differences that often arise between teachers and between teachers and parents.

SUPPORT SYSTEMS FOR TEACHERS

School leaders do best when they know something about the human ego and how it shapes the personality and behavior of teachers and students. To repeat what will be elaborated upon in a later chapter: school leaders may discover that teachers often respond to them by transferring attitudes from associations they experienced in their past life. Each individual may assign a role to the school administrator that meets her own inner need: she may come to see the administrator as a parent, former teacher, brother or sister, or simply the personification of authority inside the organizational setting. She will react to school administrators by loving or hating them, depending upon how completely these feelings fulfill her unconscious needs. Teachers may agree or argue, they may placate or tease, they may trust or test, based upon their inner perceptions of the school leader. They will only begin to act in more conscious and responsible ways when their administrators help them to reflect on their actions inside the school building.[24]

It may sound difficult, but it is not. School leaders need to know something about how the ego functions and how they can give it support. Only then can they deal with the preconceptions and attitudes that govern the motivations and behavior of teachers and students.

What is the human ego? Recent research defines it as that part of the mind that helps individuals understand and adapt to the world in which they live. This is how Heinz Hartmann and Anna Freud described the ego, and it echoes the way that Sigmund Freud first described it in his early research. Researchers have since confirmed their original findings—among other things, the ego helps people to test ongoing reality against their preconceptions; it helps them remember things; it helps them to focus their attention on particular objects rather than on a diffuse gestalt; and it directs both their conscious and unconscious behaviors.[25]

Therefore, it is important for administrators to understand the part the ego plays in governing the personality and behavior of teachers and students. To work with the attitudes of teachers and students is an important skill that administrators need to master if they are to bring shadowy thoughts and emotions into the light of consciousness where the ego can help make some sense of them. This is what is meant by training reflective administrators and teachers. Psychologists who have studied these problems believe that the ego plays an organizing role between instinctual impulses and drives and the needs of social reality. People's everyday behavior and voluntary actions are directed by this part of the personality, whose primary function is self-preservation. The ego is concerned with anxiety, anticipation, and conflicts that lead to poor associations and perceptions.

The most important need of teachers is other teachers and supervisors. Every staff member needs someone she can talk to at home and at school. This is the only way she can pause and reflect on what she is doing in her classroom and how it is being received by students. But this can only take place when the relations between teachers and supervisors are good. The bond between them needs to be constantly strengthened. Otherwise, administrators cannot acquire the information they need to perform their supervisory functions effectively. Although some teachers may seem disinterested in their work, they can become more involved if they are made more a part of things: if they are accepted even when they react to administrators in unpleasant ways. How can this be done? The "how-to" of improving communication systems in school organizations occurs when administrators commit themselves to formal, ongoing conferences. When school leaders and teachers work together in such meetings, they learn to exert inner controls over their own negative, unproductive behaviors and attitudes. The reaction of peers in group meetings, for example, can help individual teachers to redefine and rethink their attitudes and actions inside the school organization.

The following are some important ideas behind the methods that will be discussed in the next few chapters:[26]

1. Teachers (and students) do not always respond to events in a completely conscious way. Often they seem to be unaware of what is happening to them. But a basic idea of this new way of working with them is that *all teachers (and students) have complete consciousness*. They know everything that's happening to them in the classroom or school building. Often, however, their awareness is buried in what Freud called the preconscious, and they do not seem to be responding well to what is happening at a given time and place. Just below the surface, however, waiting to be brought to clear consciousness by inquiry methods, are the attitudes and insights that influence their behavior.

2. When administrators talk to teachers *they generate attitudes and emotions* in themselves and in others that are both negative and positive at the same time. With their desire to present a cooperative, competent appearance, many teachers (and administrators) ignore or repress negative emotions, hoping they will simply disappear. But these attitudes and emotions do not disappear. They persist and sometimes surface at

inopportune moments, making teachers and administrators appear inconsistent and untrustworthy.

3. *All individuals behave in ways that make sense to them,* even if the meaning of their behavior is not always apparent. Often, the motivation for the behavior is rooted in knowledge and awarenesses that are hidden from them in their preconscious. In meetings between school leaders and teachers, these behaviors should be the topic of discussion and analysis because they are often expressions of inner feelings and attitudes. What a teacher meant when she acted in a certain way is an important question to explore. For instance, the administrator might say, "What were you trying to say when you acted in that way?"

4. *The need for friendly associations is an important one* in our society and in school organizations. Teachers need someone to talk to about what is happening to them in their classrooms. Good relations are critical to the educational and psychological well-being of all members of the school organization.

5. If teachers have an opportunity to reflect, and to talk and listen to other professionals, they have an *opportunity to establish higher levels of trust and consciousness between them.* They have an opportunity to become more friendly and accepting of each other. A good school climate advances the learning process. If teachers feel alienated from the school and its leadership, they may harbor negative attitudes that usually remain shrouded in their preconscious. These emotions can make schoolwork a less pleasant activity for them, increasing absenteeism and causing unnecessary conflict in the organization.

6. To develop good relations and communication channels with teachers, school administrators need to establish more open, ongoing ways of talking to them. *They need to replace their critical attitudes with questions and an accepting attitude* that allows teachers to reconstruct and analyze their classroom activities, locate problems and difficulties and suggest solutions. If, as postulated, all individuals have complete consciousness, it is foolish to tell them what they did right or wrong in a particular lesson or situation. They already know. They know, although sometimes that knowledge is not readily available to them without the help and guidance of the facilitating supervisor.

7. One of the important benefits of providing teachers with unconditional acceptance is that *they begin to trust administrators. Teachers will then be willing to share important information with their supervisor.*

Administrators are attracted to these ideas because of the climate they create for everyone inside the school building. Four factors seem to be important: (1) trust, and the need for more friendly relations; (2) confidence, and the establishment of reflective practices as a part of the organization's formal structure; (3) warmth, and the establishment of caring attitudes that encourage teachers to listen and respond to the children they serve; and (4) acceptance of others, rooted in the idea that learning and higher levels of awareness of one's feelings are part of the same process.[27]

Typical outcomes reported by researchers are better communication channels and higher levels of confidence and proactivity among teachers. Innovation is encouraged by mutual acceptance and experimentation; new and better ways of completing schoolwork grow out of the ongoing problem solving activities that help administrators and teachers reflect upon the work they do together.[28]

Other reported outcomes are the constant upward flow of information from the teaching staff to higher levels of authority in the organization. Two factors seem most significant: (1) teachers show an openness to discuss their problems with their administrators and with other teachers; and (2) they exhibit more spontaneous behavior and present personal fronts that seem to be more in harmony with their inner attitudes and identities.[29]

Providing opportunities for teachers to talk about their work establishes two-way communication patterns that helped school leaders learn more about what was happening in their classrooms and allowed innovative school leaders to break out of the bureaucratic organizational structures that stifle communication today. Such practices permitted teachers to integrate themselves into the planning and decision making processes of the organization both inside and outside their classrooms. Decisions were now made on a more consensual basis, rather than on the misinformed hunches or perceptions of isolated school authorities.[30] Teachers were encouraged to express themselves fully, understanding that ambivalence is the normal condition of most human responses to ongoing interaction in the school organization.

Another important area of change was in the the goal formation of teachers and administrators. Four key areas are worthy of mention: (1) problem solving was institutionalized and an awareness of the needs and concerns of others intensified; (2) needs assessments were used to provide teachers and administrators with an opportunity to plan their schoolwork proactively; (3) group permissiveness, within certain predefined limits, gave teachers a greater sense of involvement in the school-wide and classroom decisions of the school organization; and (4) the establishment of mutual evaluation procedures allowed teachers and administrators to work together as co-professionals seeking to provide the best learning environments for themselves and their students.[31]

The absence of administrative support systems often leads to the defensive, directive leadership practices that exist in so many schools today. When fear, anxiety, and distrust are used to control staff, teachers become unimaginative and unproductive.[32] Studies of authoritarian practices suggest that they cause teachers to become ambiguous and less committed to their work and to sometimes distort the information they provide to administrators.[33] As a counterstrategy, teachers make things seem a little better than they really are in the classroom, or they simply avoid mentioning problem areas at all. Therefore, the school leader of the future needs to be skilled in both task and maintenance abilities. She needs to know how to organize the work of teachers and how to help them plan their classwork effectively. She needs to be able to help teachers express themselves clearly in reflective sessions that focus on the solution of work-related problems. Teachers want to do their classwork more effectively. They want to succeed with the students they serve. But they do not wish to do this at the expense of their dignity and feelings of competence; they do not wish to do this at the expense of the dignity and competence of their students.

SUMMARY

In summary, leadership research tended to focus upon the traits of leaders until World War II, when the army decided to learn more about it. The result was a series of essays that defined leadership in terms of situations, interpersonal relations, and the ability of leaders to communicate with their followers. Some researchers continued to study leadership in terms of the power and influence of leaders, focusing primarily on individuals who possessed the formal designation of leader in complex organizations. Others became more interested in the leaders' behavior, seeing it as the center and cause of much of what happened to the leader. This approach assumed that the situation was also an important player. Still other researchers continued to study the traits of leaders long after this line of research had been abandoned by mainstream researchers because leaders and followers were found to possess the same traits. Finally, following Hersey and Blanchard and others, researchers centered their attention on the situation within which leadership actions occurred. They asked what task was to be done in a particular situation and how ready the leader and followers were to perform it. This readiness factor has been called "maturity." The leader needed to assess the maturity and capability of individuals and the group as a whole when faced with specific tasks and situations. Teachers as a group may be at one level of development while individual teachers are operating at a higher level of awareness and expertise. When leaders interact with more capable teachers they need to do so differently, taking into account their maturity and readiness to perform certain organizational tasks. For instance, leaders may ask older teachers for some guidance and assign them as mentors if they seem willing to perform such tasks. When working with new teachers, leaders may visit them and meet with them frequently to help them gain the order and control they need to teach the students. When working with teachers who have been granted tenure, leaders may help them think about doing their work in more creative and rewarding ways.

Hersey and Blanchard defined maturity in terms of two related factors:

1. *The leaders' willingness and ability to establish high but practical objectives for teachers and students.* Some people were highly motivated to achieve their goals and wished to know how they were doing on an ongoing basis. Others were less task-oriented and more concerned with whether they were liked by the group's members.

2. *The proficiency and eagerness of the leader and followers to take responsibility for achieving the group's objective.* Proficiency meant having the technical information and skills needed to do the work itself. Such skills might include the ability of leaders and followers to work well with other members of the group, by listening and speaking effectively with others, solving disputes and problems, developing good interpersonal

relations, and learning good supervisory skills that emphasize mutual evaluations and trust between faculty members.

Situational leadership theory argues that (1) the capability or maturity level of the organization's members can be improved over time; and (2) that as this happens the effective leader will see a dimunition in task-oriented actions and an increase in relationship-building behaviors. As with so many other management theories, situational leadership breaks down its analytical factors into task and interpersonal orientations and behavior. When the ability level of a group or organization is low, the leader needs to emphasize tasks while placing a lower priority on interpersonal relationships in the workplace. Members at this level do not have the skills, insights, or knowledge to set goals or to take responsibility for their own actions. The leader must be more directive in such situations, telling teachers what to do, and how to do it.

But growth can occur. The leader's emphasis can change as the maturity level of group members increases. Situational leadership models, such as the Path-Goal Theory, Vroom-Yetton, LPC Contingency Model, and Cognitive Resource theories can help students begin to think about the role the situation plays in the complex relationships that occur when leaders and followers interact. Unfortunately, empirical research has failed to support the effectiveness of these leadership models. Therefore, researchers have had to pay more attention to speech and language and the roles they play in organizational interactions between leaders and followers. During the last few decades, management theory has espoused participative methods as being more enlightened and effective than the traditional directive leadership that prevailed in the United States during most of this century. This approach assumed that managers and leaders would be more effective if they received better information about what was happening in the organization during the work process.

PROJECTS

1. Interview your school principal. What type of leadership style does she use with her teachers? What role does power and influence play in the way she structures her school? How aware is she of her behavior and the behavior of others? Does she change her behavior to fit the different situations she finds herself in?

2. Write a short essay describing the way you interact with the students in your classes. What type of leadership style do you use most of the time? What pressures do you feel to act in certain ways because of the demands of administration or parents? How much help is your administrator in helping you to solve classroom problems?

NOTES

1. William R. Lassey, "Dimensions of Leadership," in William Lassey (ed.), *Leadership and Social Change* (Iowa City: University Associates Press, 1971), pp. 4–10;

Gerard Egan, *The Skilled Helper: A Systematic Approach to Effective Helping* (Pacific Grove, Calif.: Brooks/Cole Publishing Company, 1990).

2. Richard A. Schmuck and Matthew R. Miles (eds.), *Organizational Development in Schools* (Palo Alto, Calif.: National Press Books, 1971), ch. 1; B. Joyce, R. Hersh, and M. McKibbin, *The Structure of School Improvement* (New York: Longman, 1983).

3. Jack Gibb, "The TORI System of Leadership," in J. Pfeiffer and J. Jones (eds.), *The 1972 Annual Handbook for Group Facilitators* (Iowa City: University Associates Press, 1972), pp. 212–214.

4. Robert G. Owens, *Organizational Behavior in Education* (Boston: Allyn & Bacon, 1995), pp. 176–182; Stanley W. Rothstein, "Conflict Resolution in a Supportive Environment," *Education and Urban Society* (February 1975), pp. 193–206.

5. II. Hartmann, *Psychology and the Problem of Adaption* (New York: International Universities Press, 1958), pp. 6–7; Stanley W. Rothstein, *The Voice of the Other: Language as Illusion in the Formation of the Self* (Westport, Conn.: Praeger Publishers, 1993), pp. 11–115.

6. Luvern L. Cunningham, "Leaders and Leadership: 1985 and Beyond," *Phi Delta Kappan* (September 1985), p. 20; Stanley W. Rothstein, "Building and Maintaining High Trust Climates: Training the New Administrator in Feeling Expression and Inquiry Skills," *Education and Urban Society* (November 1976), pp. 81–87.

7. Harry Stack Sullivan, *The Collected Works of Harry Stack Sullivan*, Vol. I (New York: W. W. Norton, 1953); Chris Argyris, *Personality and Organization* (New York: Harper & Row, 1957); Jacques Lacan, *The Seminar of Jacques Lacan*, Jacques-Alain Miller (ed.), Sylvana Tomaselli (trans.) (New York: W. W. Norton, 1991).

8. R. Likert, *The Human Organization, Its Management and Value* (New York: McGraw-Hill, 1967), pp. 23–24; Amatai Etzioni, *A Comparative Analysis of Complex Organizations* (Glencoe, Ill.: Free Press, 1961); William J. Rothwell, Roland Sullivan, and Gary N. McLean, *Practicing Organizational Development: A Guide for Consultants* (San Francisco: Pfeiffer, 1996).

9. Rothstein, "Conflict Resolution in a Supportive Environment," pp. 205–206; Stanley W. Rothstein, "Ego Support in a Supportive Environment," *The Guidance Clinic* (February 1984); Stanley W. Rothstein, "Supportive Supervision," in Andrew E. Dubin (ed.), *The Principal as Chief Executive Officer* (London: Falmer Press, 1991), pp. 150–164.

10. Bruce R. Joyce, "The Teacher Innovator: Models of Teaching as the Core of Teacher Education," *Interchange: A Journal of Educational Studies*, Vol. 4 (1973), pp. 27–60.

11. Joyce, Hersh and McKibbin, *The Structure of School Improvement*, ch. 4.

12. Stanley W. Rothstein, *Schooling the Poor: A Social Inquiry into the American Educational Experience* (Westport, Conn.: Bergin & Garvey, 1994), ch. 1.

13. Sigmund Freud, *Civilization and its Discontents*, trans. James Strachey (New York: Norton and Company, 1962), pp. 11–22. See also C. R. Rodgers, "Reflections on Feelings," *Person-Centered Review* (1986), pp. 375–377.

14. F. Fiedler, *A Theory of Leadership Effectiveness* (New York: McGraw-Hill, 1967), pp. 245–255.

15. Gertrude Blanck and Rubin Blanck, *Ego Psychology: Theory and Practice* (New York: Columbia University Press, 1974), pp. 340–343; Sigmund Freud, *The Ego and the Id*, trans. Joan Riviere (New York: W. W. Norton, 1989).

16. Lassey, *Leadership and Social Change*, pp. 26–40; H. B. Karp, *The Change*

Leader: Using a Gestalt Approach with Work Groups (San Francisco: Pfeiffer, 1966), ch. 1.

17. Lassey, *Leadership and Social Change*, pp. 27–29.

18. Stanley W. Rothstein, *Schools and Society: New Perspectives in American Education* (Englewood Cliffs, N.J.: Prentice-Hall, 1996), pp. 139–149.

19. Ibid., pp. 150–156.

20. R. H. Hall, *Organizations: Structure and Process* (Englewood Cliffs, N.J.: Prentice-Hall, 1972), ch. 4.

21. T. Sergiovanni, "Beyond Human Relations," in T. Sergiovanni (ed.), *Professional Supervision for Professional Teachers* (Washington, D.C.: Association for Supervision and Curriculum Development, 1975), pp. 11–12.

22. David Nasaw, *Schooled to Order: A Social History of Public Schooling in the United States* (New York: Oxford University Press, 1979), pp. 22–24, 128–135.

23. Chris Argyris, "Interpersonal Barriers to Decision-Making," *Harvard Business Review*, No. 44 (1966), pp. 84–97.

24. F. Redl and D. Wineman, *Children Who Hate* (New York: Free Press, 1951), pp. 195–205.

25. F. Redl and D. Wineman, *Controls from Within* (New York: Free Press, 1952), pp. 16–17.

26. Edith Jacobson, *The Self and the Object World* (New York: International Universities Press, 1964), ch. 2.

27. Marshal W. Meyer et al. (eds.), *Environments and Organizations* (San Francisco: Jossey-Bass, 1978), pp. 21–25.

28. J. S. Bruner and P. Greenfield, *Studies in Cognitive Growth* (New York: John Wiley and Sons, 1966), pp. 1–8.

29. R. Wynn and C. Guditus, *Team Management: Leadership by Consensus* (Columbus, Ohio: Charles E. Merrill, 1984).

30. Joyce, Hersh, and McKibbin, *The Structure of School Improvement*, pp. 42–45.

31. Rothstein, "Conflict Resolution in a Supportive Environment," pp. 193–206.

32. Stanley W. Rothstein, "Researching the Power Structure: Personalized Power and Institutionalized Charisma in the Principalship," *Interchange: A Journal of Educational Studies*, Vol. 6, No. 2 (1975), pp. 41–48.

33. Jack Gibb, "Dynamics of Leadership and Communication," in *Leadership and Social Change* (Iowa City: University Associates Press, 1971), pp. 85–105.

3

Leadership Skills: Understanding Group Dynamics

QUESTIONS TO THINK ABOUT

1. Why is it important to understand the informal group structures in schools?

2. How do primary groups influence the attitudes and behaviors of individuals?

3. What are influence groups and how do they influence the organizational climate of schools?

4. What is the human ego and what functions does it perform for us?

5. Why is ambivalence so prevalent in human responses to their environments?

6. What are defensive mechanisms and how do they inhibit open communication between supervisors and teachers?

7. What is meant by group conflict?

8. Why are interpersonal relations so important in improving the organizational climate of schools?

Many school leaders know little about the group processes that shape the identities of teachers and students. They know even less about group dynamics. Yet group identities are very important in determining the perspectives and behavior of staff members and children.[1] By observing staff members and students in groups, school administrators can learn a lot about their familial identities, values, and concerns. Supervisors need to know more about group processes if they want to better understand why teachers and students talk and behave the way they do in classrooms. Only then can they learn about the deeper meaning of the behavior and emotions of teachers and students; only then can they understand why some members of their school community resist new ideas about school improvement and supervision. There is no better way to get to know the teachers and students in a school than by studying how they work in groups.

For these reasons, administrators need to study the group processes that are taking place inside the school building. Both formal and informal groups are functioning in every organization; they are the means through which individuals give and receive the social approval and support they need. It is in groups that teachers and students adapt their ideas and behavior so they conform more closely to the norms of other teachers and students, parents, and administrators. It is in groups that important social controls are brought to bear on staff and students and that newcomers learn about the school's past by seeing things through the eyes of others who have preceded them. Groups of administrators, teachers, parents, and students pass on the folklore of the school; they make newcomers aware of the prevailing attitudes that have developed because of the peculiar history of the organization.[2]

The group exists only in the speech and language of members and non-members. It has no reality of its own, no mind, no substance. Its force is derived from the speech and language of its members and the cultural history they come to share over time. The group is nothing more than the memories and emotional ties of its members and the speech and language that gives these ties meaning. Only members, interacting over time, can give the group its power and influence over their emotions and behaviors. This power is further enhanced by the status of members in the group, and in the wider society in which they live and work.

Administrators may begin their study of groups by gathering demographic data about their school populations. How large is the student body? How many children are in the average classroom? How does classroom size help or hinder the development of good learning climates? What is the physical structure of the building like? Is it functional and impersonal? Or does it try to present a more friendly face to teachers and students? What types of children does the school serve? Are they generally healthy, or do they suffer from malnutrition and other ailments associated with poverty and familial distress? What are the racial, ethnic, gender, and class issues that the school needs to attend to? And most important, what are the relationships like between teachers and students? Do they like and trust each other, or does fear and distrust dominate the associations between them?[3]

If an administrator is to provide supportive leadership and supervision to teachers and students, she will have to appreciate the importance of their social biographies, and understand how the life stories of teachers and students influence how they see themselves in the school organization. Whether teachers and students like or dislike the school will depend, in part, on their previous interactions with families and friends and on their past experiences in schools.[4] From kindergarten on to their placement in ability groups, childrens' sense of self-worth and competency has been influenced by teacher judgments and group associations. Were they in the "dummies" group, or "were they doing well in class?" was a major concern.

Group situations help administrators uncover and observe staff and student conflicts.[5] Conflicts sometimes happen in the teachers' lounge or lunchroom and provide a way of blowing off steam. But beneath the surface, group processes may play other, less positive, roles in determining how people respond to one another each day.

Administrators need to be well aware of the ideas and skills that are clustered under the heading of the group process if they are to learn more about the ties and relationships that bind or separate people in the building. Unless they acquire these insights and understandings about the behavior of teachers and students, administrators will be unable to work effectively with them; they will be unable to help teachers communicate with other staff and students.

If an administrator wants to know more about a teacher, it is important for her to see that individual through the eyes of other staff. In this way, the supervisor can see how others work with the teacher, how they react to her efforts, and how they influence her self-perceptions and sense of competence. The self-confidence of teachers and students is always affected by their contact with others in the classroom and school building. Their behavior is often influenced by group experiences and the previous identities they developed outside of school. At home, they may have had low status; in their current home situation, they may have to do much of the menial work; they may live with people who place little value on education. Every teacher and student is a different person in a different situation, with a different self-image and status. An individual may be passive, shy, and retiring at home, yet present an entirely different front in school. Teachers may be pleasant and agreeable in face-to-face meetings with administrators but critical of them in the privacy and protection of the teachers' lounge; or they may be overbearing toward the children they are supposed to serve once their classroom door is closed.

The values and beliefs of individuals are always the outcome of previous associations in primary groups. Before birth, neonates are given racial, ethnic, and class identities by their parents.[6] During prenatal and postnatal care, their health is deeply influenced by the health of the mother and the diet and medical care they receive. The newborn's first needs are those of self-preservation, safety, and social intercourse with nurturing others.[7] The customs and beliefs of parents are paramount in deciding how these needs are satisfied. From birth to age three, infants embark on a journey from the natural world to the world of humans; they learn the speech and language of their parents and adapt to the norms of family life. Parents and older siblings teach children what is right and wrong, and what is good and bad. They help them to see what they need and what they can expect from other family members and strangers.

School leaders need to understand that the values and beliefs of teachers and students were not learned in any formal sense; they are not the product of formal schooling.[8] They were acquired in constant interactions with parents and significant others and carry more weight than rational arguments or "facts." All human beings begin life in the most helpless of conditions and suffer through a long period of dependency. During these years, youngsters are deeply influenced by the social outlook and thought processes of those who care for them. Long before they acquire speech and language at about age three, infants behave in response to the thoughts and feelings of significant others. Later, as they grow older, they will maintain and strengthen these "normal" ways of doing things, especially if they are not challenged by new conditions. Most often, individuals will accept the speech, language, and thought patterns of their elders without too much thought.

ADOLESCENT GROUPS

As people mature, they often develop a need to challenge and break away from childhood norms and value systems. As infants they developed ideas about who they were and how they should behave by fulfilling the expectations of their parents. They developed a sense of themselves, an ego, which was separate and apart from others. They also developed a sense of what was "right," a superego: they learned what was worthwhile and what was not. But in their adolescent years, as people approach adulthood, they are deeply influenced by friendship groups and their own emerging needs and impulses: they find that, to establish their own identities, they must seek greater independence from their parents. Therefore the demands of parents are resisted or openly defied. Adult authority is doubted and sometimes disobeyed, even at the cost of losing the love and affection of parents. More and more, adolescents look to peer groups for adventure, approval, and support.[9]

Like the family, the adolescent friendship group develops its own code of conduct and behavior. It establishes its own values and ways of doing things. Adolescent behavior is seen as defiant by many parents. To assert their independence, youngsters sometimes move further away from their parents and hand over the power to influence their thoughts and behaviors to peer groups. In short, adolescents revolt against the demands of adults and question their motives. Adolescent peer groups ease the transition from childhood to young adulthood; they allow youngsters to share experiences with one another so as to lessen their common fears and anxieties.

Adolescent peer groups are often a catalyst for change. Youngsters learn the speech and language of the group, adapting themselves to its values and ways of doing things; they learn to change their ideas so they can fit in with other members. As they interact with others in the group, they may be influenced by the beliefs and values of group members who are more experienced in coping with the adolescent experience. Individuals learn and accept values and norms that are characteristic of their particular group. In turn, the group provides its members with guidelines and a safe haven that helps it to maintain itself and its identity or "culture."

Every group has qualifications and standards its members must meet. Every group insists that members conduct themselves in prescribed ways: they must respond to the outside world in ways that meet the approval of the group. Often, members of adolescent groups wear clothing and insignia that differentiate them from non-members and from their own past dependent status.

What has this to do with school life? Teachers and students in a school setting belong to many formal and informal groups that influence their behavior, norms, value systems, and world views. The groups affect the way teachers and students behave in classrooms; they are a powerful, yet invisible, influence in school and classrooms affairs. For example, they encourage teachers to work for predictable conditions of employment, even when this means they will continue to be isolated in cellular classrooms. They encourage staff to seek greater autonomy, even when such autonomy makes collective action more difficult. These standards require teachers to seek low surveillance: teachers tend to resist supervision, even though such behavior may alienate them from administrators and prevent them from adopting new methods of classroom instruction. Moreover, acceptance of traditional modes of organization, of cellular, self-contained classrooms pushes teachers into a paradox: as teachers become the important people in their classrooms, they become more powerless outside of them. Teachers work in comparative isolation, while administrators expand their operational spheres over management through the paperwork that links the school to the larger educational bureaucracy, the truancy records that link the school to the legal system of the state, the scheduling and timetables that control the behavior of teachers and students throughout the school day, the lunchroom and yard duty rosters that govern lunch periods, and the discipline procedures that establish the culture and morale of the school.

Influence groups force teachers to take strong positions on questions of morality training in schools,[10] and on curriculum changes that may be suggested by higher authorities. Influence groups may prod some teachers to work for school integration, for example, even when this policy goes against popular opinion. In other instances, they encourage thousands of teachers to join professional organizations and unions, even when such actions place them in opposition to other teachers, administrators, and community groups.

Their group norms can force teachers to view supervisors as management personnel whose boss-oriented leadership needs to be resisted vigorously. Teachers will take such positions even though they tend to separate them from other teachers and school administrators. Moreover, such conflicts may spill over into the everyday activities of the organization: as teachers become more socialized into their professional roles and identities, they sometimes tend to move away from older norms, values, and identities; they accept the newer definitions and ideas of influence groups. But the strength of their old allegiances deeply influences the degree to which they can alter their ideas and commitments.

HUMAN PERSONALITY

Many administrators have little knowledge of depth psychology and the impulsive systems that govern much of human behavior. They believe such matters have little relevance to their work in the organization. But the impulsive systems of individuals deeply affect their behavior in and out of schools and need to be studied by serious administrators. Ego Psychology, the foundation upon which all the helping professions rest, can be of help here. Researchers have pointed to two important human drives: (1) self-preservation, and (2) participation in family and social life. Based on their observational research, they report that in the first moments of life, the neonate, or newborn infant, is consumed by her need to survive. All the baby's instincts and energies are used to communicate her need for food, warmth, and comfort. The neonate's focus is entirely upon her needs and her survival as a living being.[11]

Later, the neonate begins to notice others who come to her side when she cries or calls for them. She learns that her needs are satisfied by a nurturing figure, and that they sometimes go unsatisfied when she is not heard. If the neonate finds herself in a loving, supportive environment, she can turn her attention to other matters and interact more fully with others in her family circle. Her progress develops from these first demands for sustenance to new behaviors that are more complicated and related to her development of speech and language. Effective communication in primary groups depends upon the neonate's ability to create some balance between satisfying her impulsive needs and responding to the demands of her social situations, between giving and taking. Because satisfactory growth is achieved when the neonate has attained a sufficiently strong ego or control structure to organize her behavior, the development of an inner control structure is an essential prerequisite for group building in families and the evolution of the infant's self-concept.

Administrators can think about human personality more easily if they focus their attention on two fundamental areas: (1) the impulsive system, and (2) the ego or control structure.[12] The impulsive system is made up of the drives, urges, impulses, and needs that force individuals to behave in ways that gratify them. It is controlled or contained by the ego, which has the responsibility of selecting and modulating the individual's responses to the social world. In the past, some researchers had postulated that some control functions were lodged in a superego or conscience. But more recently, researchers have subsumed this superego into the ego itself, describing it as simply another example of the way in which inner controls are exerted by individuals.

To repeat, then: human personality grows impulsively, in the beginning. But as the neonate begins to respond to the power and strength of group standards and the norms of her family, she develops a control structure, or ego, of her own. This structure helps her to establish contact with others so she can satisfy her own needs for self-preservation and social intercourse. Moreover, it helps her to predict what a particular encounter will be like before it happens, and it helps warn her of behaviors that might evoke social disapproval and danger.[13]

Out of this struggle between the newborn's impulsive needs and the controlling force of the emerging ego, the infant develops a unique personality. Because many of the newborn's impulsive needs might meet with disapproval and rejection by her parents and other family members, she often represses them, pushing them out of her consciousness. But they do not disappear. Rather they remain within the preconscious or unconscious and cause the newborn to behave in ways she often does not fully understand. This is another function of the healthy ego: to identify and appraise what is happening inside one's own mind. Some of the newborn's impulses are pushed out of consciousness or are not conscious to begin with; some are not even known to the ego, either on a conscious or unconscious level. Of course, the ego cannot control what it does not know about. Therefore a second important function of the control structure is to help people know themselves, so they can better control and rationalize their perceptions and behaviors. This is an important concept: it is at the core of Heinz Hartmann's *Theory of Neutralization*, which will be discussed in the next chapter.[14]

The development of the neonate's personality is, therefore, an interplay between the impulsive and control systems. The neonate is deeply affected by her interactions with members of her primary group, learning their speech, language, and culture by the age of three. At this time, yet a third function of her ego, or control structure, can be observed: it makes her more aware of the values and demands of family members. It helps her to identify and control behaviors that would go against their beliefs and ways of doing things, providing her with an appraisal of her own emerging conscience.

The practice of enlightened school leadership is based upon an understanding of these mental processes as they influence the individual and group life of members of the organization. The administrator needs to understand that the power of a person's ego sometimes does not go beyond helping her think about what she ought to do in a particular situation. School leaders need to be able to help such teachers act in accordance with such insights through the practice of supportive school supervision.

AMBIVALENCE

A school leader who wants to become skilled in the process of communicating with, and accepting, staff members should be aware of the nature of human ambivalence.[15] The neonate emerges from a perfect environment in which every need was satisfied automatically. She enters the world traumatically, beset by elemental needs that cannot be fully satisfied or denied. Her need for social intercourse is a primal need, and she experiences satisfaction from her first contacts with the nurturing other. From the first moments of life, the newborn's feelings are a mixture of pleasure and pain, loving and hating, accepting and rejecting. Researchers report that the infant stares at the mother's face, especially when she is feeding at the breast. She learns to associate her mother's face with the satisfaction of hunger needs. But the satisfaction may be delayed, making the infant frustrated and upset. The infant's positive and negative feelings are called forth each time she feels that her needs are not met. Still, being human, her wants are insatiable; a sense of deprivation persists in even the most carefully nurtured infant and child.

The neonate is able to feel positive and negative emotions at the same moment, during the same experience. Throughout later life, she attempts to satisfy her need for acceptance and love; she strives to control her impulsive nature and negative reactions to others. But people who do not learn to verbalize positive and negative emotions are often unable to understand or control them. The individual needs and desires the warmth and nurturing behavior of a loved one. When she is unloved, she feels deprived and lonely. But her associations with parents, friends, and lovers have taught her that aggressive, angry behavior pushes others away from her. She is afraid that even those few who care will stop caring if she acts in ways they might disapprove of. Therefore, her anger and sense of deprivation are confounded by a new, more complicated emotion: anxiety. Then the mechanism of the ego helps her to contain behaviors and emotions that might be harmful to her or to those she loves.[16]

The child learns to use the unconscious as a receptacle for anxiety-provoking material. Often, this material is kept outside of the awareness of the ego control structure. Unfortunately, the material that is unknown to the self can be known to others because of the behaviors that result from unconscious impulses.

RESISTANCES

It is important for school leaders to know something about how people resist when they feel themselves endangered by others in individual and group conferences. Some teachers try to suppress their more aggressive emotions because they would be embarrassed and upset by the responses of others in the group. These teachers try to eliminate unpleasant attitudes from their behavior, while others offer elaborate rationalizations for their negative and unresponsive attitude toward school life.[17]

Administrators often sense free-floating anger during their first meetings with teachers. Staff members often seem nervous and on guard; they interact in formal, detached ways that seem to show a disinterest and disaffection with the organizational life of the school. Such teachers may respond defensively to questions or compliments, sending confusing and contradictory messages to other educators or students. In private, these teachers may admit that they do not like or trust school administrators as a group, that they believe administrators "speak with a forked tongue."[18] Every staff member has a different way of dealing with supervisors and defending herself against real or imagined attacks. Some teachers use the rationalizing powers of the ego to explain away conflicts and emotions, thus ignoring their validity. Others sublimate their emotions and direct their energies into more acceptable behaviors. Sometimes sublimation provides the teacher with a substitute satisfaction: instead of expressing her frustration and anger, she overreacts or engages in behaviors that provide her with substitute gratifications.

Other times, teachers may use another defensive response, symbolization. In these cases, unacceptable impulses are transposed into artistic efforts or creative lesson plans. Symbolization is believed to be responsible for much of the music and art that has been created during the long history of humankind on this planet. Moving antisocial attitudes into other mediums of expression often results in an acceptable social response. Sometimes, fine arts and creative educational efforts can help individuals work out their problems.

A teacher who is not aware of her own motivations may sometimes use displacement as a way of dealing with problems. She may direct her anger at an administrator or fellow teacher rather than at the real source of her resentment. She may also project some of her feelings onto others in the organization, ascribing to them her own feelings and attitudes.

Such defensive responses by members of the school organization are merely attempts to fit into formal and informal groups. Very often, as the following example shows, they are normal reactions to the directive leadership that is so common in many school organizations today:

Today, the principal asked me to witness a meeting with Mr. Brown, a teacher he is not very happy with at the moment. Mr. Brown entered the principal's office with a frozen smile on his lips. Apparently he was aware of what was about to happen to him. After seating himself, he waited for the principal to finish writing something in his notebook.

"Do you know why I sent for you?" The principal was sitting forward now as he finally looked up at the teacher. On his desk, he had a notebook in which he recorded what was happening during the meeting. This began to look very serious, indeed.

"No, no. As a matter of fact, your note didn't say why." Legs crossed, hands firmly clasped, and arms cradling one another, the teacher's posture seemed to suggest extreme defensiveness. His fingers moved constantly; his face was tense and his voice thin. He seemed to "know" what to expect in meetings like these. Perhaps he had experienced them before or heard about them from other teachers.

"Well, I won't beat around the bush. There have been complaints about you. Lots of them. And about your classroom, too." The teacher sat quietly in his chair. He made no reply. Rolling his eyes toward the ceiling, the principal went on in a more exasperated voice. "Your fellow teachers say you are unable to control your classes. Parents are also complaining about shouting, running, and noise. It upsets the entire school when one weak teacher can't keep a lid on his class!"

"No one ever said anything to me. Why didn't they come to me?"

"Maybe they thought it wouldn't do any good."

"I'd like to know who these people are."

"I can't give you their names. But I can tell you I've passed your room several times this week, and your classes are very noisy and disorderly."

For several seconds, no one spoke. "You mean you were outside my room and didn't come in to see what was going on? Wouldn't it have been better to see for yourself? I don't remember being visited by you at any time during the school year."

The principal scribbled something in his notebook.

"You may not like the way I do things, but the fact is that I did pass your room and I do know what's going on there. Everyone in that part of the building knows! They know and I know! You have no control over your classes. The kids are running wild! And I want it stopped! Stopped!''[19]

Four perspectives can be used to analyze this meeting: the suppositions of the teacher and principal before the action began, their perceptions once the situation began to unfold, the mood of the conference, and the feelings that developed between the two men during the meeting.

When entering a principal's office, a teacher's behavior is often influenced by her assumptions about what is going to happen in the meeting. As the meeting progresses, both the teacher and the administrator are influenced by their perceptions of what is happening. The teacher's nervousness seemed to indicate that he knew how he should behave in the situation. He was on the defensive from the moment he entered the principal's office. The information that forced him to assume such an attitude was part of his social knowledge of the organization, which had been learned from others and from his own past experiences in schools. He knew in advance that he would have to defend himself in the principal's office. The principal also possessed social knowledge about these kinds of encounters. He knew that, as the administrator, he possessed the decisional rights in the situation. Such rights allowed him to ask teachers to his office to speak to them about things he felt to be of importance. His advice, evaluation, or warnings almost always evoked defensive responses from teachers. In this encounter, the teacher tried to defend himself by asking questions: "Why didn't they come to me?" "Who are these persons?"

The mood of this confrontation was "serious" because both men knew this was an evaluation session. The administrator had the power to evaluate and dismiss this untenured teacher. Had the teacher reacted in inappropriate ways, he would have surely been reprimanded, and he would have expected such a reprimand.

After this meeting, both the teacher and the administrator were able to identify the suppositions they had when the action began. The principal felt a certain need to assert his authority. But he was displeased by the teacher's initial responses. He could not see that his lack of empathy for this new teacher contributed to the teacher's defensiveness, and he would not accept the idea that evaluation almost always evoked similar responses from teachers. He was surprised to learn that the teacher had negative feelings about him and about the way he had handled the situation. The teacher felt the principal was attacking him and forcing him to defend his teaching practices. Yet he wasn't surprised by such behavior. He had learned something of what might happen by talking to another teacher who seemed to know what was going on. The teacher felt the evaluation was unfair because the principal had not taken the trouble to see what was happening inside his classroom. This didn't surprise him, however, since "nobody ever sees this principal in the classroom."

ACCEPTANCE

To each schooling situation, the staff person brings her unique personality, the result of her social biography and upbringing. She joins informal groups because she wishes to associate with other teachers who are having similar experiences or who appeal to her in other ways. Because of her appointment to the position of teacher, the newcomer is usually accepted by the teaching staff[20] but she is not automatically accorded acceptance and status. These may come later when she has developed close ties and proven her ability to "control her classes," or they may come at the first meetings and then slacken off as she becomes better known. However, within the informal groups that form in every school organization, administrators can observe certain patterns of acceptance or rejection:

1. The *loners*, or outsiders, come to every meeting alone and usually keep to themselves. They sit off to one side and are seldom spoken to by other teachers. When committees are formed, they are usually not selected to serve on them; they are ignored or talked about disparagingly by teachers when they are not in attendance. These teachers are isolated people who are experiencing a severe form of social rejection; they have few, if any, warm spots they can turn to during the school day. These individuals may be shy and retiring, or aggressive and uncooperative. In either case, the teaching staff is deprived of their contributions as long as they are allowed to continue in this excluded condition, as long as they are unable to break out of their isolation. To assist such teachers, the administrator should move toward them and seek to learn more about them and the problems they face in the school. She should seek out information that will help her understand what is going on and how she can integrate them into her teaching staff.

2. *Buddies* come to every faculty meeting with the same co-worker. Everyone knows that they are friends outside of school and inseparable inside the building. When voting, they usually vote as a bloc, and they always select the same committees to serve on. They are a twosome, a pair. Their inclusive relationship tends to exclude everyone else, arousing some anger and aggressiveness in other staffers. Their friendship is satisfying for them but much less so for others who are left out.

3. The problem of analyzing acceptance in interpersonal relations in school organizations is often complicated by a prevalent lack of *trust*. Trust means more than mere predictability of behavior. It implies friendliness and mutual regard, while distrust carries with it attitudes of unfriendliness and nonacceptance. In many school organizations today administrators are seen as outsiders, or worse. They are the center of suspicion and resentment, especially when they first begin their work in new schools. Teachers wonder, What are their intentions? Will they be able to help them in their classwork or will they become part of the problem? To reassure staff, administrators should develop interpersonal and communication skills so they can be more open and responsive in their communications with others. Such skills can help them learn more about their staff so they can ascertain whether the behavior and statements of teachers are merely performances or a true reflection of their inner inclinations and identities.

Teachers perform their organizational roles not as actors but as persons with names, needs, and feelings. To know when their behavior is a true representation of their inner feelings requires more personal relations with them. Only in this way can trust be encouraged between teachers and school administrators.

GROUP STRUCTURES

Bonds between people in families are important because they have a decisive influence in structuring the self-concepts and value systems of individuals. School leaders should be aware of the characteristics of primary groups such as families:[21] (1) They are long-lasting and constant in their membership: people are born into them or belong to them as they belong to a family; (2) they may be formal or informal; (3) they rely upon a division of labor among their members; (4) they develop behavior patterns and member interactions that symbolize their particular group; (5) they establish traditions and ways of doing things that are known only to members; (6) they interact with other groups and individuals, thus establishing themselves in more complicated social settings; and (7) they tend to develop a group spirit or élan that glorifies unified thought and action. Some primary groups are consciously formed so that members can strengthen their ties with one another, but these tribal feelings are not as strong as family ties. The natural, or primary group, however, is based on family and extended family bonds and usually predates any experiences in work organizations.

Secondary groups, on the other hand, are aggregations such as school organizations, where teachers are recruited for classroom work and other duties. Such groups always lack the strength and permanency of primary groups. According to Ferdinand Tonnies, in *gemeinschaft*, or primary groups, unity is essential and continues even when members are far apart; in *gesellschaft*, or secondary groups, separatism predominates, even when members are united in a common effort to secure organizational goals.[22]

Group structures in school organizations constantly change, as do the relationships of their members. Informal and formal mechanisms regulate the behavior of teachers and students inside the building. Group structures provide organizational members with the norms and privileges that come with membership. Administrators can map these informal groups and trace their interactions by asking certain questions: Who are the leaders? Who are the followers? Whom do they follow? Why? Who are the solitary people who don't seem to belong to any group? Who are the negative people, the nay-sayers?

Researchers have used two polar types to study group interaction patterns in complex organizations: conflict and accommodation.[23] Conflict refers to behaviors that express opposition to group efforts and goals, while accommodation is a process of consensus-seeking and group-building. Members can react to group behavior in one of two ways: (1) they can leave, disassociating themselves from group statements and actions; or (2) they can cooperate with others. Although teachers are required to participate in group life in their classrooms and school organizations, many are reluctant to do so with peers with whom they might feel some discomfort. These staff members need to be helped to participate in schoolwide planning enterprises. Any attempt to improve the quality of a school's climate needs to begin with the formation of formal groups committed to a process of school improvement. This can only been done by teachers who enter into the group life of the school and accept the increased responsibilities and more formal organizational needs. In this way, the purposes of the organization be realized and collective action and proactive planning can determine the working experiences of teachers and students. To achieve a united, consensual climate, administrators need to make certain that teachers participate in decision making processes that affect them in their everyday classroom work. In such an environment, supervisors are able to see and hear the needs and concerns of teachers, learning firsthand about the differing values and problems of staff members.

Often the disagreements between teachers in consensual environments force them to find new approaches to their conflicts. The solving of problems can be approached in many ways. One method is for administrators to ask teachers how their working situation would look if they were able to structure it to their satisfaction. Then the variance between what is, and what ought to be, can become the basis of problem solving activities. Strategies can be devised to close the gap between the real and ideal situations.

The problem becomes more complicated once interpersonal conflicts arise. Opinions can stiffen, or become more accommodating, as the group seeks consensus. Some members may try to dominate others, trying to have their ideas adopted no matter what the majority of teachers feel. This can even reach a point where individuals and factions that are against them are targeted for expulsion from the group. Dictatorial members may even force others to agree to things they oppose in principle. However, if there are strong personalities in the group, a process of compromise may begin, during which concessions are made by competing individuals and cliques in order to secure group stability and cohesion. Sometimes groups of dominant persons may merge themselves in a temporary arrangement to strengthen their efforts to achieve important common goals. At other times, decision making may take the form of unanimous consensus: everyone agrees to a plan of action that seems most suited to solving an important organizational or group problem. When this happens, the group has reached the highest level of integration and solidarity that it can achieve.

School administrators should observe teachers as they struggle to decide things together, as they work to solve the problems they face in common.[24] They must be aware of what can happen when staff come together outside their classrooms. Inevitably, there will be conflicts. Teachers are accustomed to having their own way in their classrooms where they are the important decision makers. Administrators should observe teaching groups to see if there are any obvious clashes, especially when spending and budgetary items are discussed.

GROUP CONFLICTS

The health of an organization, or other group, depends on its ability to generate friendly feelings and trust and to lessen feelings of unfriendliness and distrust.[25] Teachers need acceptance, support, and empathetic regard. When these needs are not met, staff members tend to operate less efficiently. Effective groups consist of individuals who are well disposed to one another, who have recreated the climate of the family structures of their first years. Like brothers and sisters, group members may bicker and fight. When they are threatened from without, however, they come together to protect one another. Like functional families, effective groups have a deep affection for all members and a sense of oneness that may make them intolerant of criticism from outsiders. As a result, some groups may separate themselves from other teachers inside the building. Segregation can become a serious barrier to communication and professional growth, depriving teachers of needed outside input and stimulation. It can become a way of excluding other staff members, thus generating much resentment and hostility from outsiders.

The administrator needs to understand that expressions of fear, anger, and anxiety are just as normal and necessary as those of trust, contentment, and friendliness. She learns this by studying the nature of human ambivalence and by investigating her own values, norms, and preconceptions. She learns that, in her own youth, the concepts of good and bad were firmly implanted in her mind by parents. She also learns that others have their own preconceptions, and she accepts this. By using her previous education and experience, the administrator comes to see and appreciate others who have different cultural backgrounds from her own. She learns that some of the behavior of teachers is caused by their previous associations and understandings about school organizations and administrators. She begins to appreciate their anxieties and resentments. She begins to understand that one of her important tasks is to encourage teachers to express their feelings openly and constructively.[26]

Helping teachers to express themselves is part of the leadership process in school organizations; it is an outgrowth of everything that happens to a teacher from the moment she begins her teaching career. In her first meetings, the administrator is the authority person; she represents the interests and concerns of the entire school and community organization. Working together, the supervisor and staff influence each other's outlook and behavior. As a result, their policies are modified, especially as they affect the goals and purposes of specific classrooms.

The school leader needs to understand that she becomes part of the group when she meets with teachers; she becomes part of their problems and later solutions.[27] Perhaps for this reason alone, a supervisor needs to become more aware of her own actions and prejudices, her own stereotypes. She could begin this process by examining her reasons for accepting the administrative position in the first place. Why did she choose to leave teaching? What are her reasons for bringing staff members together in groups? Why does she want to supervise their efforts, and what skills does she bring to this task?

The school leader needs to become more aware of the group standards that influence her behavior. By becoming more conscious of these norms, she can begin to see how they influence her work with staff members. By becoming more aware of the way that fellow administrators demand conformity, for example, she can better appreciate her own actions and the responses of teachers. No one wants to be the center of negativity in an organization; no one wants to violate the rules and norms of the administrative or teaching staff in a particular school district or school.

Staff meetings are sometimes characterized by conflict because teachers bring different values and standards to them. They use preconceptions about other staff members to decide what their initial responses should be; or they use ideas about themselves to formulate their present goals, instead of reacting to the ongoing situation. If participants do not respond to what is happening at the moment, staff meetings turn into futile struggles for power. Endless arguments about how to do things and "what is really important" cause the group to accomplish little.

Many administrators have become aware that meetings for the planning of pedagogical and curriculum matters are made even more difficult by the following types of staff behavior:[28]

1. In some faculties there are one or more individuals who try to dominate the others. These teachers try to solve problems by "walking over others," by forcing other teachers to submit to their will. Such actions invite others to (a) struggle to eliminate the opposition, (b) "subjugate" the opposition, (c) form pacts with others to defeat the opposition, (d) seek an accommodation of some sort, or (e) co-opt and integrate the ideas of opponents into a new or different group consensus. All of these responses were identified by behavioral scientists more than a generation ago. They are defensive responses that carry with them heavy loads of confusion and anger. None of them helps the faculty or school leadership function effectively.

2. Some members simply submit to the domination of others without attempting to make their thoughts or feelings known. In response, other teachers may rely on their own projections, which are sometimes governed by their own anxieties and unexpressed emotions, to guess the emotions of the silent members. Why aren't these quiet ones making a contribution? Why aren't they doing their share? Is their lack of involvement a sign of disinterest? Of disagreement? Of anxiety? Or are they simply unwilling to let others know what they believe, what they think the staff should be doing?

3. One important insight about the group process is worth reiterating: it functions best when staff compromise their differences and accommodate willingly to the consensus of the group. Even so, the motivation of negative individuals needs to be explored and understood. Their perspectives and reservations need to be verbalized and, when necessary, defended by administrators against the sanctions of other group members who are afraid to deal with conflict. Simple observation techniques can help. There is a need to see who talks to whom, in what manner, with what intended effect, and

with what actual outcome. A sociogram can help the supervisor understand the status of individual teachers in the informal school organization: Is she a leader or follower? Is she popular or isolated?

4. Supervisors should observe how groups of teachers make their decisions. Are there dominant members, or do teachers participate together in determining the purposes of the group? Every group provides members with different demands and situations. Different skills and understandings are constantly called into play. Do new informal leaders arise to deal with new conditions? Or do the formal leaders always act in leadership roles, even when there are others who are more knowledgeable or qualified to perform particular tasks?

5. Administrators should study which teachers have more status than others and why. What is the basis of their rank and prestige? Does it have to do with professional skills, or are social skills more important? These insights into the structure of teaching staffs are often overlooked. But supervisors need this information if they are to better understand why staff members act as they do. Moreover, more sophisticated organizational skills are needed when supervisors begin to work with larger faculties. However, in general, merely observing what is happening in a group meeting can help administrators learn a great deal about their staffs. Seeing teachers as members of formal and informal influence groups can help the supervisor become more empathetic toward them. Perhaps the supervisor has emphasized surveillance and evaluation in her efforts to get staff to improve their classroom practices. Such supervisory attitudes force staff to fall back on old defensive ways of responding to inspection-oriented supervision. Teachers do not want to make mistakes; they do not want to be given poor evaluations. Surveillance only closes the lines of communication between teachers and supervisors, making for a climate that is governed by anxiety rather than trust.

To repeat, then: a supervisor's success in working with teachers depends mostly on the types of relations she develops with them. When an administrator is inconsistent and bossy, teachers quickly sense that she is not someone they can come to with their problems. A supervisor has to be responsive to the needs of staff members. This will cast her in the role of a caring person, someone who listens attentively to their cares and concerns. To successfully project a responsive image, school administrators need to be aware of the informal group structures that exist in the organization and how to use them to develop better learning climates for teachers and students.

SUMMARY

It may be most helpful to think of the role of the administrator as one of inquiring facilitation.[29] Teachers need supervisors who listen and respond to their needs and concerns. A major reason for restructuring school organizations is so teachers and supervisors can meet with one another regularly. The "how-to" of successful administration needs to be accomplished in weekly meetings that provide supervisors and teachers with the information and insights they need to respond intelligently to organizational needs and conflicts. If a teacher is given the opportunity to talk about her classroom activities, her supervisor can help her to close the gap between present conditions and those that are more desirable. Together they can begin to identify and solve the problems that exist just below the surface of her consciousness. Only when teachers have an opportunity to express themselves openly can administrators begin to deal with some of the deeper problems that exist in the organization.

A problem solving system needs to be put in place if supervisors are to deal proactively with what is happening in their schools. In a recent study it was reported that one characteristic of such systems was essential to its success: the weekly individual and group conferences that gave supervisors and teachers an opportunity to reflect upon their practices and problems.[30] In these meetings, teachers were encouraged to think about their own actions and those of their students, to listen attentively, and to act in accordance with the insights they developed in these reflective sessions.

This method of problem solving relied upon the relations between administrators and teachers; it also depended upon the relations between staff members and students. This is important because the questioning techniques used in these sessions can be seen as the "third degree" if relations between supervisors and teachers are poor. The key to the success of this method was the trust and friendship that developed between teachers and supervisors, which determined whether teachers saw the questions as an effort to provide them with supportive supervision or as an intrusion into their organizational space.

School leaders need to become more aware of their feelings toward the teachers with whom they work. Like all human beings, supervisors may like and dislike people at the same time. But the negative feelings of supervisors are often denied or ignored, even when they seem obvious to others. Therefore administrators need to make a special effort to be more aware of their feelings toward individual teachers. They need to learn to use themselves in a more conscious way, verbalizing their attitudes in order to increase their own levels of consciousness. Only in this way can the rationalizing power of their egos, or control structures, come into play. Without this raised consciousness, supervisors will almost surely send double messages to teachers; they will behave in inconsistent and seemingly arbitrary ways; and they will find that teachers begin to trust them less and less.

PROJECTS

1. At your next faculty meeting, observe the groups that seem to form there. Who comes with whom? Who comes alone? Who talks to whom before the formal meeting begins? Then draw a sociogram of what you have seen. Who are the informal leaders of the staff? Who are the loners? Who is listened to once the formal meeting begins? Who seems to be ignored?

2. Think about your own life. How has your family influenced your attitudes and behavior? What can you remember about your earliest years that seems significant to

you? How closely do your thoughts and feelings resemble those of your parents? How much do they differ? Write a few lines answering these questions. Are your attitudes toward those in authority influenced by your earliest experiences in your family?

NOTES

1. A. Blumesteil, *Acquaintance: Structural and Relational Features of Laboratory Training* (unpublished dissertation), pp. 178–183; C. R. Bell, *Managers as Mentors: Building Partnerships for Learning* (San Francisco: Pfeiffer, 1996), pp. 122–124.

2. Stanley W. Rothstein, "Teachers and Students in Urban Schools," in Stanley W. Rothstein (ed.), *Handbook of Schooling in Urban America* (Westport, Conn.: Greenwood Press, 1993), pp. 189–194.

3. D. C. Kinlaw, *Coaching for Commitment: Managerial Strategies for Obtaining Superior Performance* (San Francisco: Pfeiffer, 1996), pp. 200–203; Jack Gibb, "The TORI System of Leadership," in Jack Gibb and K. Benne (eds.), *T-Group Theory and the Laboratory Method* (New York: John Wiley and Sons, 1964), pp. 25–29.

4. Stanley W. Rothstein, *The Voice of the Other: Language as Illusion in the Formation of the Self* (Westport, Conn.: Praeger Publishers, 1993), pp. 1–23.

5. F. Hesselbein, M. Goldsmith, and R. Beckhard, *The Leader of the Future: New Visions, Strategies, and Practices for the Next Era* (San Francisco: Pfeiffer, 1996), pp. 12–15; R. J. House, "A Path Goal Theory of Leadership Effectiveness," *Administrative Science Quarterly* (September 1971), pp. 321–338.

6. Stanley W. Rothstein, *Schooling the Poor: A Social Inquiry into the American Educational Experience* (Westport, Conn.: Bergin & Garvey, 1994), pp. 92–95.

7. G. Blanck and R. Blanck, *Ego Psychology: Theory and Practice* (New York: Columbia University Press, 1974), pp. 40–73.

8. M. S. Mahler, *On Human Symbiosis and the Vicissitudes of Individuation* (New York: International Universities Press, 1968), pp. 6–15.

9. Harry Stack Sullivan, *The Collected Works of Harry Stack Sullivan*, Vol. 1 (New York: W. W. Norton, 1953), pp. 263–312.

10. H. B. Karp, *The Change Leader: Using a Gestalt Approach with Work Groups* (San Francisco: Pfeiffer, 1996), pp. 66–67; K. D. Benne and P. Sheats, "Functional Roles of Group Members," in *Group Development* (Washington, D.C.: National Training Laboratories, 1961), pp. 51–59.

11. Blanck and Blanck, *Ego Psychology*, pp. 128–131.

12. F. Redl and D. Wineman, *The Aggressive Child* (Glencoe, Ill.: Free Press, 1957), pp. 58–62.

13. H. Hartmann and R. M. Lowenstein, "Notes on the Superego," in *The Psychoanalytic Study of the Child* (New York: International Universities Press, 1962), pp. 42–81.

14. Jacques Lacan, *The Seminar of Jacques Lacan*, Book II, ed. Jacques-Alain Miller, trans. Sylvana Tomaselli (New York: W. W. Norton, 1991), pp. 20–21.

15. E. Jacobson, *The Self and the Object World* (New York: International Universities Press, 1964), pp. 60–63.

16. Jacques Lacan, *Speech and Language in Psychoanalysis*, trans. A. Wilden (Baltimore: Johns Hopkins University Press, 1989), pp. 263–268.

17. Richard J. Altenbaugh, "Italian and Mexican Responses to Schooling: Assimila-

tion or Resistance?'' in Stanley W. Rothstein (ed.), *Class, Culture and Race in American Schools: A Handbook* (Westport, Conn.: Greenwood Press, 1995), pp. 91–106.

18. From my field notes.

19. From my field notes.

20. David Johnson, *Reaching Out: Interpersonal Effectiveness and Self-Actualization* (Englewood Cliffs, N.J.: Prentice-Hall, 1981), pp. 171–194.

21. Stanley W. Rothstein, *Schools and Society: New Perspectives in American Education*, (Englewood Cliffs, N.J.: Prentice-Hall, 1996), pp. 1–5.

22. F. Tonnies, *Community and Society*, trans. C. P. Loomis (East Lansing, Mich.: Michigan State University, 1957), pp. 65–74.

23. R. Maurer, *Beyond the Wall of Resistance: Unconventional Strategies That Build Support for Change* (San Francisco: Pfeiffer, 1996), pp. 32–34; G. E. Wiley, ''Win/Lose Situations,'' in J. Jones and W. Pfeiffer (eds.), *The 1973 Annual Handbook for Group Facilitators* (San Diego: University Associates, 1973), pp. 105–107.

24. Rothstein, *The Voice of the Other*, pp. 121–126.

25. From my field notes.

26. H. Hartmann, *Essays in Ego Psychology*. (New York: International Universities Press, 1958), pp. 1–6.

27. J. J. Murphy, *Pulling Together: The Power of Teamwork* (San Francisco: Pfeiffer, 1996), pp. 188–191; J. Haley, *Problem-Solving Therapy* (San Francisco, Calif.: Jossey-Bass Publishers, 1976), pp. 3–7, 33–34.

28. From my field notes.

29. Sigmund Freud, *The Ego and the Id*, trans Joan Riviere (New York: W. W. Norton, 1960), pp. 63–66.

30. Stanley W. Rothstein, ''Conflict Resolution in a Supportive Environment,'' *Education and Urban Society* (February 1975), pp. 193–206.

4

Basic Interpersonal Skills for Leaders

QUESTIONS TO THINK ABOUT

1. What are the four basic skill areas associated with establishing better interpersonal relations in schools?

2. Why is it important for school leaders to express themselves in clear and unambivalent ways?

3. How can school leaders build support systems for teachers and students?

4. Why should school leaders establish communication systems between themselves and those they serve?

5. What is meant by self-disclosure?

It is only saying the obvious to say that situations demanding interpersonal skills abound in the public schools. The creation of a good organizational climate that encourages cooperation and trusting associations between people should be an important priority for any school leader. To do this, administrators must pay attention to the types of relationships that develop inside the school organization. How personal are people willing to be in their associations with others? Does anxiety or trust dominate the way people communicate? How well do teachers and administrators listen and respond to each other? How willing are they to help when things are difficult? And, finally, how effectively do teachers and administrators resolve the conflicts and problems that arise in their working relationships?[1]

Teachers sometimes shy away from becoming "too personal" or "too friendly" with school administrators or with other teachers. They may not want to tell others too much about themselves for fear of rejection. They may have been taught to think of self-awareness as an unpleasant search into the more upsetting aspects of their personalities. They are afraid they will not like what they discover about themselves; they are not sure they will accept themselves "as they really are." But high levels of trust can only be achieved by establishing relationships in which individuals get to know each other. This requires a specific skill: the ability to self-disclose about things that are happening in working situations with others. This is difficult to do and requires practice. It can be done best by administrators and teachers who have developed some degree of self-awareness. Such people are more conscious of their inner attitudes; they are less likely to send double messages when they speak; and they are less likely to act out of unconscious impulses.

A second important skill is that of communication, which is closely related to self-disclosure.[2] To communicate effectively, administrators must convey their thoughts and feelings clearly and unambiguously. This skill contributes to the establishment of good school climates; it is important in providing an accepting workplace for teachers and students. Working with teachers and students generates both positive and negative attitudes. Teachers may become angry, confused, frustrated, disappointed, anxious, envious, and bitter; or they may become fulfilled and elated as they interact with others in the school organization. Very often, negative emotions are repressed, for reasons that will be discussed in a later chapter. This is not helpful and usually leads to inconsistent behavior by administrators and teachers.

School leaders should consider communication and trust-building important skills they need to master. Self-disclosure should be embraced because it provides administrators and teachers with important information about what is happening in the schools and classrooms. With this knowledge, administrators can take more intelligent steps to solve school problems. Accurate and unambiguous efforts to "see the other's point of view" should be seen as a way of becoming more empathetic to every individual in the school organization. With this supportive environment as a base, school leaders can undertake schoolwide activities more confidently. Moreover, they can count on teachers helping one other in difficult classroom situations.

When an administrator tries to build better ties to a particular teacher, she needs to pay attention to the norms and values that are developing in their conferences. Norms provide teachers with ideas about how such meetings should be conducted; they are preconceptions about what is, and is not, appropriate in the situation. The more formal the relationship between an administrator and teacher, the less likely that either will trust or support the other wholeheartedly; the less likely they will be to depend upon each other in difficult circumstances. Building better relationships is important for school leaders and requires insights and skills in four areas: (1) self-disclosure, (2) trust building, (3) acceptance, and (4) providing mutual support for everyone in the school organization.[3]

When a teacher self-discloses to an administrator in an angry voice, she is calling out for someone to understand her feelings. She is asking for attention.

When she is encouraged to talk freely about what is bothering her, the administrator (and the teacher) learn more about what is really happening inside the school building. They learn where "each of them is coming from." They begin to develop better relations with each other. The school leader can use these moments to help the teacher reflect upon the problems she is having in her classroom or elsewhere in the school. The "how-to" of such helping relationships will be discussed in the chapter on the supervisory process. By providing acceptance and regard, the supervisor allows the teacher to concentrate her energies on understanding what she is doing in her classroom and to what effect. The effective supervisor provides a climate that centers upon problem solving activities and focuses the energies of teachers and administrators on identifying and solving classroom difficulties.

Administrators can benefit by learning more about the process of ego-building. Because human beings almost always develop in a dyad, disturbances in interpersonal relationships can best be understood by referring back to the ways in which individuals learned to delay impulse gratification in infancy.[4] The process of *neutralization*, or control of one's impulses, begins early in life and is discussed more fully in Chapter 5. The ego, or control structure, of an individual is established and made secure through experiences with frustration and satisfaction, which are all accomplished within the framework of family life and constant interaction with a nurturing person. As the child learns the speech and language of her parents, she passes from the animal to the human sphere of existence. Everyone needs someone to talk to, someone they can count on, someone who is important to them in some way. This suggests a central focus for school leaders: communication systems must be in place if teachers are to reflect upon the services they provide to students and to begin to identify and resolve difficult interpersonal and educational problems inside the classroom or school organization.

To establish positive communication systems in the school, the administrator's attitude and behavior must be predictable. The administrator needs to be there, in the same mood and responding to teachers in the same way, each day. Pressure to conform to preferred bureaucratic norms eases somewhat in this type of atmosphere. Defensiveness is minimized. Teachers can now deal with their own anxieties rather than wasting energy on feelings of frustration and anger with their working conditions and supervisors. The positive attitude and skills of the school leader provides opportunities for teachers to strengthen their inner control structures. Aggressive feelings can be discussed as the first step in neutralizing them. Otherwise, these emotions remain embedded in the preconscious or unconscious where they cannot be dealt with effectively.

Teachers often become less tolerant of frustration when they work in schools that succumb to the impersonality of mass organizations. They tend to vent their anger when administrators are not around, unaware that they are not completely conscious of their own emotions and the impact of these emotions on their work. The behavior of teachers becomes more inconsistent and unpredictable because no one is helping them move from the active to the reflective stage of doing their work. They have no one to help them see and understand more fully their own successes and difficulties.[5]

SELF-DISCLOSURE AS A LEADERSHIP SKILL

Self-disclosure has been defined by researchers as an individual's ability to talk openly about herself.[6] To communicate effectively, people must be able to talk about their thoughts and feelings truthfully. The more an administrator knows about herself, the more she can communicate that information to others. The more a teacher or student knows about the leader's thoughts and feelings, the more they are able to understand her motivations and actions. School administrators and teachers have to be accessible to one another and to the children they serve; they have to be individuals who can be approached easily. They have to be the ones others want to talk to about their problems inside the school building.

Moreover, the school leader's ties with staff are further strengthened when she is conscious of her own impulses, attitudes, and stereotypical thinking.[7] To communicate clearly, administrators need to be able to disclose themselves truthfully. Only then can they begin to talk meaningfully to teachers and students. Only then can they appreciate and accept themselves and the people with whom they work. When a supervisor is unable to do these things, she generally finds herself alienated from the teachers and students in her school. This limits the amount and quality of information she can gather and affects her success as a school leader and an individual. Poor school leadership weakens ties between teachers and administration and decreases school morale. An estranged supervisor can never gain the trust and affection of her staff, nor can she feel positive emotions for them. Effective communication requires good interpersonal relationships so that supervisors and teachers can know how they are thinking and feeling about each other and about what is happening in the school. How can a teacher respect, accept, and confide in a school leader she knows little about? How can an administrator appreciate and respect a teacher she does not know? Good relationships are essential to school morale and staff effectiveness. A truly successful leader has spontaneous and truthful associations that encourage staff to self-disclose so they can come to know their own feelings more clearly: so they can make contact with one another and with the children with whom they work.[8]

If an administrator is unable to talk about herself, she cannot become close to the teachers and students she serves. She cannot establish a communion with them that grows out of their shared responses to ongoing experiences inside the school. Since disclosure is an essential link in developing trust and friendliness, it is not surprising that administrators and staff who choose to remain silent about themselves are often strangers to each other. Knowing oneself is the first step in getting to know others; it requires self-understanding and self-respect.

Knowing another staff person is the second step in establishing meaningful communications and ties; it requires listening and responding to teachers and students in order to understand them better.

When supervisors share their responses to ongoing events with staff, they are disclosing the basis for their administrative decisions. This helps teachers understand the associations that develop inside the building. When a teacher is able to talk freely with her supervisor, she develops an ability to reflect upon their relationship and the incidents that are taking place inside the school building. A teacher's verbalization of attitudes about ongoing events helps her socialize her impulses and feelings. This form of self-revelation deals mostly with the present. It seldom involves disclosing occurrences from the teacher's past. To sensitively elicit such confessions is beyond the training and skill of most school administrators. To do so might create a false sense of closeness and trust, but these feelings would be transitory at best. Nevertheless, when a supervisor wants to build a good relationship with a teacher, she must encourage mutual disclosures about feelings and reactions to experiences in which both are presently involved.

Good relationships are based on acceptance and understanding that develop from information that school leaders and teachers disclose to each other. The repression of such information only increases the tension and sense of separation both feel during their work together. It distorts their ability to understand what is happening between them, making it more difficult for them to provide each other with the information both need to function effectively. As with other forms of suppression or repression, an individual usually hides her feelings because she thinks others will not like her if the truth becomes known; she thinks that others will become angry, upset, and defensive.

Self-revelation is an important and difficult skill for administrators and teachers to master. How they can accomplish it and still maintain a professional relationship is an important question. To summarize, then, the following are some things a supervisor should be aware of, as she attempts to build healthy relationships with her staff:

1. The more a supervisor confides her reactions to staff, the more they will understand, accept, and support her.

2. An administrator is more likely to reveal her feelings to a staff member she likes and trusts.

3. If a supervisor engages in self-disclosure, teachers are likely to communicate to her their true feelings about ongoing situations.

The revelations between supervisors and teachers should be appropriate to the level and intensity of their relationship, and they should focus upon the ongoing work process. During the initial stages, supervisors should be careful not to disclose too much too soon. Teachers may be frightened away by such behavior.

Healthy relationships are built gradually and go through a series of stages that establish the bases for intimacy and trust.[9]

When supervisors disclose effectively, they do so within the context of an ongoing association that thrives on communication and is reciprocal in nature. Often administrators and teachers want to make sure they are understood. "The reason I did that . . ." usually is one way they begin to self-disclose. "I am angry with you," is another way they talk about their feelings. Both persons want to know how things are going between them; both want to be sure the other knows their intentions. This provides administrators and teachers with important insights that can be used to improve things between them. Before a good supervisor does something, she thinks about how staff will react if she behaves that way. She becomes more conscious of herself and the people around her, and she provides a climate that makes more personal and meaningful relationships possible.

There are times when a supervisor should not self-disclose: for instance, when a teacher is unfriendly or untrustworthy. Without the support of a friendly and trusting association, teachers and students often misinterpret what a supervisor says and does. They can impede the flow of communication by reacting in overly hostile or fearful ways.

Administrators do a lot of talking—such as telling others what they should and should not do, and interpreting new directions from higher authorities. Yet few have been trained in disclosing information that will help teachers and students know and appreciate what they are doing. To engage in genuine self-disclosure, a supervisor has to be secure and accept her own thoughts and feelings. To be effective, an administrator must be aware of her own impulses, urges, emotions, and thoughts. Only then can she hope to communicate with teachers, parents, and students effectively. Researchers have found that people who are unaware or unaccepting of their own feelings and behavior seldom self-disclose effectively to others. Such people have trouble communicating; they have poor self-concepts and tend to distort what others are saying and doing; and they are often insecure and fearful about their own emotions and those of others with whom they work. They tend to have trouble talking to others and find it almost impossible to admit they are wrong when they make a mistake.[10] People who do not accept their own feelings tend to react to constructive criticism as if it were a personal attack on their identity and the authority of their office. In their insecurity, they move further away from their co-workers because they feel unworthy and incompetent. Hiding feelings inevitably leads to isolation and loneliness because feelings can never be hidden completely.

FEEDBACK

Giving feedback is another important leadership skill.[11] Yet few supervisors do this consistently; few provide information that helps teachers to understand how they are doing in their classrooms on an ongoing basis. Many school leaders don't seem to understand how important such feedback can be; they don't look for new ways to get feedback, and they don't spend enough time reducing the defensive responses of those they serve. The more threatened a teacher becomes, the more likely she will be to distort what is being said to her. Therefore, school leaders need to become adept at giving supportive, non-threatening feedback and at encouraging others to give them such feedback as well.

What is non-threatening feedback? First and foremost, it is focusing attention on what the teacher said or did in a particular situation. To do this, the teacher must be separated from the observed behavior so she hears only what was said or done. The administrator does not judge the teacher or speculate as to why she did and said what she did. Only the teacher can explain this. First the supervisor should let the teacher tell the story in her own words. Then she should reflect back to the teacher what she saw and heard during the teacher's story. The administrator should never judge or interpret the behavior described by the teacher or draw conclusions about what was said or done. Learning to give such feedback requires the ability to focus on a description of what was seen and heard. Feedback should be communicated without judgments, inferences, or interpretations. It requires a time frame that deals with the here and now, rather than the past, and it is most effective when it is given as soon as possible after an event has occurred.

Surprisingly, it is not commonly understood how most people, including teachers, dislike receiving advice from others. Teachers much prefer to have supervisors focus their feedback on ideas and information rather than on emotions and interpretations. Then they can pick and choose whether an idea or suggestion is right for them without having to deal with their deeper feelings and the relationships in their classrooms. Feedback provides staff with a way of identifying and solving ongoing problems. It does not solve the problems, however. There are many ways to teach, and feedback can only help teachers choose methods that suit their personal styles, preferences, or situations. Therefore, when school leaders provide feedback, they should think of its potential usefulness for the other person. An administrator has to limit the amount of information she gives to a teacher until their relationship has improved enough so messages can be accurately received and accepted. The administrator must be conscious of the moment when feedback is given. Is it the best time, the time when the other person is best able to hear what she is saying, or should she wait until a later moment?

One way to give feedback is to use the newspaperman's five perspectives: who, what, where, when, and how. These five guidelines can help the school leader provide proper feedback to staff. The important thing is to avoid trying to tell the other ''why'' she did what she did and what she meant to say when she behaved as she did. This is information that the observing supervisor cannot know for certain; only by skillful interviewing and feedback can a climate be established that encourages teachers to verbalize their inner feelings and thoughts about classroom situations without fear or defensiveness.

To summarize, when a supervisor wants to communicate more effectively with her staff, she must know something about herself; she must be aware of her own motivations and intentions. Her ability to know herself is deeply affected by the way others treat her in ongoing situations. If she is a warm, friendly person who talks openly about herself, she will tend to receive open and truthful feedback. If she is unfriendly, vindictive, or angry, others will probably be wary of telling her things about herself she needs to know. To develop good relations with staff members, a supervisor has to send clearly understood messages that she has received feedback and intends to act on it.

When supervisors learn and practice the basic skills of interpersonal expression, it actually improves their relationships with teachers and others with whom they work. Such skills help them to share their hopes, anxieties, and intentions; they learn to ask others for feedback and accept it gratefully. Moreover, effective supervisors change their behavior when it seems to be working against their goals and personal relationships; they modify their actions and statements so they more nearly reflect what they are saying and doing in different situations.

When staff withhold their true feelings about classroom events, the school leader is deprived of vital information. This happens when teachers are afraid of being rejected or misunderstood by their supervisors. Some may become shy and unresponsive in supervisory conferences; others may spend a lot of time talking behind the administrator's back; and still others may simply leave the school at the first opportunity.

Obviously, then, it is important for school leaders to understand the conditions under which constructive self-disclosure and feedback is possible. Most teachers begin to self-disclose when they feel safe and comfortable with the idea that this is a good thing to do. As a rule, they want to establish a good relationship with their supervisor first. Therefore, developing a climate in which supervisors and teachers can verbalize openly is important. Teachers must also have the "right" to resist coercive questioning that seeks to force them to "change their ways" to fit a predetermined mold. Sometimes, because school leaders are not aware of their teachers' feelings, they are not discussed at all. Talking about something soon after it happens may not be an easy thing to do in today's crowded, busy schools, but it is important to do so whenever possible. Such discussions help school leaders and teachers understand each other better and teach them to analyze what was said and done in particular settings so they can improve their supervisory and teaching practices. Conferences should be both as specific as possible and exploratory in nature. Listening skills, which check to make sure the other is being heard correctly, can help a great deal. So, too, can eye contact, posture, and echoing techniques that paraphrase or repeat what the teacher or supervisor has just said.

Even when administrators master all of these skills and refrain from judgmental and accusatory remarks, they still may not succeed in their work. This is because the ties that a supervisor has with her teaching staff can color every remark and interchange between them. When relations are good, teachers feel they are being helped by conferences. When relations are bad, they often feel that questioning and listening techniques are nothing more than a benign way of manipulating them.

So we can ask again: Why bother to learn and master such skills of interpersonal expression? For one thing, researchers have shown that leaders who have such skills are more competent and effective.[12] For another, such leaders are easier to get to know and more flexible in their dealings with others. They are more adaptable to the changing circumstances that characterize so much of contemporary work in schools. Moreover, such leaders can respond more intelligently to organizational pressures and conflicts because they have more and better information upon which to base their decisions. They are more aware of what is happening in their schools and classrooms. Finally, the constant feedback that accompanies self-disclosure provides supervisors with an opportunity to improve how they respond to others around them.

Therefore, supervisors should consider seeking out and encouraging open, truthful disclosures so they can learn more about what is happening in their schools. The soil that good relationships flower in is nourished by openness, mutual acceptance, trust, and friendliness. Open communication means listening and speaking in ways that make it easier for teachers to talk about how they are reacting in classroom situations. What was said and done in a particular situation? What were the feelings these statements or actions caused in those who were involved in this problem encounter?[13]

Open communication needs to be based upon mutual acceptance and respect between school leaders and their staff. A supervisor should not become judgmental or angry with a staff member when she learns what is truly happening in the classroom. Otherwise such communications will stop, and relations between the supervisor and teacher will deteriorate. School administrators who accept and support staff after they have self-disclosed can expect their relationships with faculty to become stronger over time. Therefore, it is very important to develop knowledge and skills in interpersonal relations. Such skills are based upon a supervisor's ability to express acceptance for an individual, while disapproving or disagreeing with something she has said or done. "I like you, but I don't like what you are saying (or doing)," is one way of expressing this idea. Such openness risks an angry or rejecting response, at first. But later it can lead to an understanding that one cares enough about the other to tell the truth; that one wants to build a relationship built upon mutual respect, support, honesty, and unconditional acceptance.

COMMUNICATION SKILLS

There are many different ways an administrator can send a message to a staff member. She can frown, speak in a harsh or angry voice, or be ominously silent. She can smile, speak in a soft and accepting voice, or be expectantly silent. Her posture may say one thing, while her spoken words say another, or she may send one consistent message to the teacher. All these ways of communicating have one goal: they seek to make contact between individuals. Usually, school administrators and staff members take turns sending and receiving such messages; they take turns communicating. All speech and behavior has intentionality, and all communications have content that transmits feelings and ideas. The sender usually translates her ideas and emotions into words and gestures, filtering them through the understanding and stereotypes of her mind. Then she sends a message that the other person can understand. The receiver has to hear and decode what has been said; she has to pass the communication through the screens of her own mental processes to understand the meaning of a particular message.[14] There can be much confusion when people try to talk to one another. School administrators and teachers have different roles and responsibilities in the school organization; they have different perspectives and concerns. Therefore, misunderstandings can easily occur between them.

When a supervisor sends a message to a teacher or counselor, three things determine how well she will be understood. First, if she has not earned the respect of the staff person, if she is not trusted, the message may be distorted by the receiver. Second, if she is not in control of her impulses or has trouble verbalizing thoughts and feelings, the message may not be understood as it was intended. Third, if she is insensitive and fails to notice the impact of her message on the other person, the effectiveness and clarity of the message may be decreased.

Fortunately, a skilled person can send messages which are likely to be understood as they were intended. One way to do this is to send the message through more than one channel. The transmission, "I like you and the work you are doing," can be communicated in words, gestures, eye contact, body language, or through repetition of the same message in different words. If the staff member is unfamiliar with the background or exact nature of a particular problem or communication, she can be filled in on these matters before the supervisor sends her the message. It may be necessary for the administrator to make the teacher or counselor more aware of the differing opinions and perspectives of parents, students, or others affected by the situation.

The clarity of a supervisor's message is enhanced when she uses words and phrases such as "I feel," or "My thoughts are . . . ," which accept responsibility for her expressed ideas and emotions. Congruent gestures, eye contact, behavior, and voice are essential if the staff member is not to be confused by the supervisor's verbal statements. This is one reason why administrators should try to adopt predictable behavior in their dealings with staff and parents. Predictability is a significant factor in establishing the one variable which is absolutely essential to effective communication: the interpersonal relationship between the sender and the receiver. If the staff member doubts the trustworthiness of the administrator, she will tend to distort the supervisor's statements and intentions. If she doubts the supervisor's expertise, she will pay less attention to what is said. This is illustrated in the remarks of many staff who tend to distrust administrators: "School administrators speak with forked tongue," is the way it was humorously expressed by one veteran teacher. An administrator's perceived predictability, consistency, and supportiveness have a lot to do with increasing her credibility.

When an administrator says something to a staff member she obviously has something to tell that person. She has a reason for speaking. If she has knowledge and skills in human development and personality, she will try to be open and truthful when discussing meanings and motives behind a particular statement or action. When such transmissions are expressed in friendly ways, the receiver can drop her defenses; she can listen to the message without putting a lot of energy into protecting herself from real or imagined threats.

Communication often reaches a higher level when supervisors encourage teachers and counselors to give feedback; supervisors learn how their words and behavior are affecting people they are trying to influence. During this kind of two-way communication, administrators and staff can monitor the consequences of their messages and change them to clarify their intentions; they can begin to work together in a more cooperative and conscious manner. Two way communication is lacking in schools where supervisors tell staff what to do, and when to do it, by flooding them with memos, reports, requirements, and speeches. This increases the separation between supervisors and their staff and makes it difficult to determine how communications are being received (and acted upon). Of course, through simple observation, administrators can get some idea about how teachers and counselors are responding to their messages. Do they seem bored and disinterested? Annoyed and upset? Are their facial expressions distracted, or are they involved in what is being said to them? Do they sit with their arms and legs crossed in a defensive posture? Do they exhibit a certain tenseness in their gestures and movements? When they speak, are their voices relaxed and confident, or do they tend to sigh a lot and speak in strained, unnatural tones? Such nonverbal feedback can be used to guess how others are feeling and responding. But the skilled leader will use observations only as a starting point; she will wait until staff tell her how they are feeling about things. And she will know that truthful answers will not be forthcoming until a good and trusting association and two-way communication have been put firmly in place.

LISTENING AND SPEAKING

Sometimes a supervisor thinks before she speaks; other times she doesn't consider the effect of her words. Without a common background or frame of reference, staff are certain to misunderstand what is being said to them. Unskilled communicators jump from one idea to the next or fail to relate ideas to one another. As a result, they are often misunderstood. Too many ideas presented in one message also places roadblocks in the way of the sender's intentions. The failure to assimilate and understand the sender's thoughts and feelings may prevent listeners from developing new insights and skills. Attentive listening can often help supervisors to get a better idea about the needs and concerns of staff at a particular time. Unfortunately, many supervisors do not listen to others with attention and concern. They are too preoccupied with the thoughts they want to express, the information they want to impart. Often, this means that the administrator and her staff are talking at each other, and may miss the essence of their communications.[15]

Attentive listening is an important part of relationship-building. How an administrator listens and speaks to staff members determines whether they will become more friendly and trusting, or more impersonal and fearful, in their associations. If a supervisor attends to what is being said to her, she draws closer to the speaker; if she is personal and deals with what is happening to both of them in the present, she draws still closer.

Often, listening and speaking skills relate to comprehension. The listener asks for clarification or paraphrases what she thinks was said in a message. This sends an important transmission to the speaker: the responder cares enough to make sure she understands the intentions of the message. The important factor remains the relationship between speaker and listener. If it is good, the listener is seen as a helpful, caring person; if not, she is someone who is "using a listening technique" to control and manipulate the speaker.

When supervisors sit down with staff to evaluate their efforts, they often increase the distance between them. During these meetings, neither person may be in the mood to communicate her true feelings and thoughts; both may be too concerned with defending themselves or justifying their actions to hear each other clearly. Even when the supervisor states clearly that she approves of the teacher's work, the evaluation session itself establishes the unequal status of the two professionals: it makes teachers and counselors aware of their inferior and dependent condition. Moreover, if the supervisor has strong feelings about how the staff member is doing her work and expresses these feelings, she may cause the teacher or counselor to further distort what is being said. Effective communication occurs when the supervisor understands that telling deprives the staff member of opportunities to explore and reflect on her own behavior and intentions. Questions, on the other hand, when asked within the framework of a situation which is jointly perceived as a helping one, allow the staff member's internal control structures to do their work: to deepen her understanding of the reasons behind her own behavior and its impact on others. Questions help the supervisor get a better idea about where her staff member is coming from in a particular situation. Paraphrasing or echoing what has been said is an effective way to decrease mutual anxiety and defensiveness.

How should administrators go about the important task of listening with warmth and empathy? Most messages a supervisor sends are meant to convey her intentions or desires. These transmissions are complex and sometimes rooted in unconscious needs and impulses. In everyday life, teachers and counselors are selective about what they hear, and attend to, in their talks with supervisors.

This is both good and bad. It is helpful because it allows both the supervisor and the teacher (or counselor) to focus on school concerns and organizational problems; but it also makes it more difficult for both of them to attend to the behavior and feelings which are affecting them.

Often, a message is distorted by the receiver's suppositions and anxieties about what she thinks is going to be said or done at a meeting. Sometimes a staff person's need for support influences the way she hears things. At other times, previous life experiences, values, and beliefs come together and affect her interpretation of the supervisor's message. Without developing a good relationship with the staff person, a supervisor can never know when some of these factors are influencing or distorting her message. If a teacher or counselor sees administrators as unfriendly, untrustworthy persons, such feelings will surely influence her perceptions and understandings. Conversely, when administrators and staff have good feelings about each other, they tend to forgive mistakes and interpret messages in ways that are supportive and friendly. Effective administrators understand that the concerns and needs of staff deeply affect what they see and hear.

Researchers have found that supervisors like people who are like them;[16] they like people who think like them; they like people who agree with them. It is much easier to communicate with like-minded persons. Yet school leaders have to work with many people who disagree with their opinions and attitudes. A skilled administrator must understand that it is easy to misperceive what naysayers are up to; it is easy to disapprove of them. But effective listening and speaking skills require her to move toward negative people to find out more about them and understand their motives. Only if she learns about them can she develop friendly, accepting ties with them.

Supervisors talk a lot, but they seldom talk about who they are, or what they are thinking and feeling at a given moment. They seldom share with others how they are responding to their position as the giving person in the school. Yet personal statements are the only way that staff can get some idea about who the person is behind the mask of the administrative role player. They are an important way of increasing friendliness and trust in a school. Personal statements give teachers and counselors a better idea about why the supervisor "does what she does." In addition, they help to assure that misunderstandings will be clarified by mutual questioning of each other's messages and intentions.

RELATIONSHIP BUILDING

Relationship-building statements are important ways of establishing closer ties between supervisors and the staff they serve. It is hard work for administrators to use these forms of communication; it is difficult for them to talk about how they think and feel about things. After all, they are supposed to be cool and competent at all times. In addition, personal statements at times can be confusing and troublesome to others, especially if relationships are poor. Furthermore, the more aware a leader is about what is really happening in a relationship with a staff member, the better able she will be to do and say things to build deeper levels of trust and intimacy. Therefore, when supervisors speak, they must clarify what they are thinking and feeling; and they must help staff to do the same so that more meaningful ties can be established.

How should supervisors speak and act if they wish to build relationships? To repeat, they must develop a climate in which mutual trust and support are encouraged. They must talk about themselves and their relationships with staff members. This means using communication skills to clarify intentions; it means reacting to the messages of others in ways which show empathy and understanding. Having spoken to staff in ways which emphasize personal statements, administrators can then take a further step. They can respond to teachers or counselors in ways which recognize and praise, in an ego-specific way, particular strengths and abilities. "I really like the way you didn't become discouraged when Johnny didn't catch on to division right away. Wasn't it good that you were able to remain patient? Isn't he lucky to have a teacher who cared enough to wait until he understood what you were trying to teach him?"[17]

The effectiveness of responses is influenced by the intent and phrasing of the sender's messages. The intentions of the message make staff aware of the supervisor's attitude toward them: they are capable or incapable; they can, or cannot, identify and work through their problems. The phrasing of a supervisor's message further clarifies her opinions and attitudes. When a supervisor responds by judging the work of staff, she complicates the communication process. These statements may be made with the best of intentions, but they create dependency and defensiveness in others. The supervisor has sent a message she may not have intended: the remarks or behavior of the staff person are subject to her constant scrutiny and evaluation.

When administrators try to explain to staff what their problems are and how they can solve them, they may intend to interpret and teach. However, the receiver gets another unintended message: she is not capable of understanding or thinking through her problem. The implication is that the administrator, who was not involved when the actual problem occurred, is better able to understand and explain things than the staff person.

The same denial of the staff member's ability and feelings occurs when an administrator tries to minimize the feelings of anger, fear, or anxiety the staff member expresses. The supervisor means to show her empathy and support; she wants to reassure the other. But the staff person, who may be expressing her feelings with some trepidation, may receive another message: the supervisor is saying her feelings are unimportant or unreal.

When supervisors respond to staff with understanding, they help them identify and resolve their own problems with a minimum of advice and interference. They use their relationships with teachers and their interview skills to help staff see all the aspects of a problem situation. Supervisors can help teachers verbalize feelings about the people they work with, and they can ask teachers to guess how others feel about them. This provides a clue: their actions and responses evoke feelings from others which they may not be fully aware of. To answer such questions accurately, the teachers will have to get to know their co-workers and students better. This need, as well as other insights, often helps teachers and counselors to begin the process of resolving interpersonal conflicts and other problems.[18]

How the supervisor responds to another's message can never be labelled good or bad in itself. The controlling variable in all communication is the relationship between the sender and receiver. When the administrator responds in the same way to many different messages, reactions are bound to be negative. Staff will wonder whether she is really listening and if she has anything of importance to offer. Therefore, it is important to use listening skills well. The supervisor should know when, and with whom, it is appropriate to respond in certain ways. She must be constantly thinking about what type of response will best strengthen the ties she wants to build with her staff.

When administrators use questioning strategies, emotions often reach a high level of intensity, especially if the relationship between the supervisor and staff member is not good. Why is the administrator asking for more information? What will she do with this information once she has it? Will she use it to help or hurt the staff member? These are some of the questions staff ask themselves. The use of questioning allows the supervisor to hide her feelings and identity behind an umbrella of queries which force teachers and counselors to respond again and again.

When supervisors and staff come together for the first time, they are curious and concerned. What will the new administrator be like? Will she like me, or will she disapprove of some of the things I do? Can we become friends? The first statements and behavior of a supervisor should deal with these concerns. Both supervisors and staff have to give each other information about the important question on everybody's mind: Will we work together in trust and harmony, or will there be conflict and fear? In this stage of relationship building, the supervisor should respond to staff by assuring them she understands what they are trying to say. She can say, "I see," or "I think I understand," or she can nod her head frequently to assure the other she is being heard and understood. In contrast, she could listen in the traditional way, with an ear toward evaluating the efforts and behavior of the staff member. She could opt for fear and distrust.

When an administrator wants to understand a message she can say, "Tell me more," or "Are you saying that . . . ?" These phrases or questions provide staff with an idea of how well they are being heard. They give staff a chance to explain, and amplify. By retelling their story, staff may gain new insights into their own behavior and become aware of angry and aggressive impulses for the first time. Teachers may reformulate their ideas and feelings and identify deeper, more significant, conflicts and problems. If feelings are good, these ways of responding will make staff feel that their supervisor is a caring and helpful person: someone who has a clear understanding of what they are trying to accomplish; someone who cares enough to accurately hear and respond to them. This helps the leader see things through the eyes of a co-professionals; it gives her another point of view about what is happening inside the school.

Supervisors have many opportunities to use understanding responses. Every time they meet with a teacher, counselor, or student, to make sure they understand a key message, they need to clarify the other's statements as much as possible. Sometimes they may miss an important point or add something which changes the sense of the message. Sometimes, by relying on their own experience and understanding as a guide, they may interpret the message. Whenever a supervisor responds to a teacher's message by telling the teacher what her message meant, she makes accurate communication more difficult. Competence in these skills can only come from practice and feedback from helpful others. Formal training can be of some help, but in the long run, each administrator will learn the responses that work best for her, and success will always be linked to the determining variable of the friendly and trusting ties she has established with staff members.

FEELING EXPRESSION

People learn to like and dislike one another in infancy; they form ideas about what is good and bad in earliest childhood. Strangers are treated with suspicion. Family and friends are accepted and liked because they share similar value orientations and experiences. Even in families, however, ambivalence and suppressed negative emotions are inevitable.[19]

To maintain friendly ties, administrators have to meet with staff frequently and learn more about them. Administrators and staff need to work together on common tasks so they can better understand each other's values. In this way, they can become aware of the things they have in common. The need to share thoughts and feelings with another person is at the core of all efforts to establish trust and intimacy. In associations which lead to greater friendliness and acceptance, both persons let each other know their thinking; they convey the idea that they like each other. Of course people like those who are liked themselves and react badly to those who reject or dislike their thoughts and behavior, as has already been stated. Being able to tell another that she is liked and respected is an important skill which supervisors should master. This is best done by facial expressions, gestures, bodily postures, attentiveness, and warmth, and by conveying a sense of empathy for what the teacher is saying and for who she is as a person.

The ability to transmit to another one's feelings of regard not only contributes to the relationship-building efforts of administrators; it is essential if effective communication is to be established between supervisors and the staff they serve. Working with teachers and counselors in this way helps them to realize their common goals. Such insights help staff and supervisors accept each other's beliefs and behaviors and to become more personal and amicable in their associations. Climates of acceptance and support require personalization and a familiarity with the language of acceptance.[20]

There is much evidence that expressing feelings can be a messy as well as a rewarding experience. Open communication channels often serve to release many unresolved and repressed feelings. As Georg Simmel taught almost a century ago, conflict is a useful warning signal that something is going amiss in the organization or small group.[21] It has to be expected. Consequently, supervisors have to know how to deal with periods of stress. The expression of angry and aggressive impulses and feelings are necessary and useful in developing more honest and insightful relations with others. Because aggressive, angry feelings have been repressed over the years, they often surge to the surface when communication channels are first opened. When supervisors deal with these feelings skillfully, they often improve their ties with their staff.

Evidence suggests that expressing feelings is constructive, necessary, and important to the health and psychological well-being of supervisors and staff members alike.[22] Open expression of feelings is difficult but rewarding. Closeness and better relationships are predicated upon a supervisor's willingness to deal with this level of human experience.

Finally, as has been mentioned earlier, it pays for administrators to encourage such expressions so they can react to situations in informed and intelligent ways. Unresolved and unneutralized feelings cause difficulties in relationships. If the staff person is to hear without distortion, these feelings will have to be dealt with in a more constructive manner. It is common for administrators, teachers, and counselors to deny feelings or not give them the attention they deserve.

Supervisors, teachers, and counselors have trouble dealing with the impulsive side of their own natures. They are more comfortable with facts, rational thoughts, and behavior. Their entire training has been factual and rational, and they are uncomfortable and unskilled in expressing feelings.[23] Educators are often more comfortable talking about the behavior of others than about the feelings behind those behaviors. They are more comfortable discussing the feelings of others than their own emotions and intentions.

Why do educators find it difficult to express feelings? For one thing, such disclosures carry with them the risk that others will reject them or respond in other unfriendly ways. Such self-disclosure also sends an unspoken message: "I care enough to tell you these things about myself and about you. I want to be your friend. I care enough to risk your anger and possible rejection." The obvious danger is that the receiver's reaction will be negative, or that she will reject the sender and her message completely. When supervisors share their feelings with staff, they lose some control. They cannot manage the responses of a teacher or counselor at this level of communication. The expression of feelings is complicated further by the fact that many do not know or accept their true feelings. Their inner control structures are unaware of some of the content in their impulsive system and so are unable to control or express these feelings constructively.

In our society, children are are taught to control their emotions at an early age.[24] Few children are taught to verbalize their emotions and impulses; few are taught to work on their interpersonal communication skills. Their parents are overly preoccupied with the competition which takes place in and out of schools. Many Americans believe that a person is more purposeful and productive when she thinks and behaves in logical, mechanistic ways: when she suppresses or ignores feelings and impulses.[25] However, in reality, people become more productive and purposeful in their work and personal lives when they are given a chance to deal with everything that is affecting their lives; when they become aware of their impulsive system's needs and drives; and when they verbalize their conscious and unconscious feelings so their egos, or control structures, can function effectively. Then, they are less likely to send unintended and ambiguous messages; they are more likely to be consistent and congruent in their behavior and communications; and they are more likely to build relationships which are characterized by trust, acceptance and friendship.[26]

Unresolved or unknown feelings lead to distortions and miscommunications between the sender and the receiver. The receiver tends to see things in accordance with her own suppositions and stereotypes. If she dislikes the sender or supervisor, she may see threats where none are intended; she may feel defensive; unneutralized feelings make a staff person less aware of her own messages and behavior and less able to see or hear others effectively. She sees barriers where none exist; she sees unreasonable responses and statements because she is unaware of the unintended and provocative messages being sent to others.

A supervisor cannot deliberately communicate feelings of which she is unaware. However, she may unconsciously transmit these feelings to others. Before feelings can be used in a constructive way to build friendships, they need to be known and accepted. Yet few administrators are aware of how their unknown and unaccepted feelings confound and confuse their expressions and behavior.

Take the situation of an administrator who is angry with a staff member and unaware of her anger. It may seem to her that the obvious is being said when she labels the staff person a "weak-link," but this is one way her lack of sensitivity affects communications between people in the school. Teachers and counselors often react to such messages with a variety of unresolved and unexpressed feelings, such as humiliation, anger, shame, embarrassment, defensiveness or hatred. An unskilled administrator may express herself in ways which produce an unintended and undesirable result, as the following shows:

Record #1

The union called for a one-day work stoppage. When I heard about it on my car radio I was confused and deeply troubled. P.S. 123 was staffed by conservative old-timers. Their faces remained passive and emotionless as I asked one and then another whether they had heard about the stoppage and what they intended to do about it. None of them intended to do anything. None of them would honor a picket line. I began to feel very much alone. The ideas with which I had been brought up were now causing me great discomfort, and I talked to anyone on my floor who would listen to me. With a union, we would receive better wages and working conditions, I told them. One of our needs was a lunch hour longer than twenty-five minutes. A second was for a better student-teacher ratio. Thursday morning, as these thoughts preoccupied me, the clerk sent me a message. The principal wanted to see me at once. With my class standing in the school yard, I seated myself on the bench outside her office and waited. The clerk assured me a substitute teacher had my keys and was meeting my class.

Then I was ushered into the principal's office. The angry accusations began at once. They came from an upset principal who accused me of organizing her school and threatening teachers who disagreed with me. When I protested, she ignored me and kept asking why I had come to her school. Why was I doing this to her after all she had done for me? Was I a union organizer? Did I really think I could get away with threatening her teachers? Did I realize she would have to send my name to the district superintendent? Did I know I might be fired? That striking was against the law in this state? That I would never be considered for tenure? That I would never receive an administrative promotion? This went on for some time. However much I denied her accusations, they were repeated in new words and phrases. When it was all over, when there were no more threats to be made, I got up slowly from my chair and walked to the door. She asked me where I was going and what I was going to do. I replied: "I'm going to join the union. I need protection from vindictive principals like you!"

The messages sent by this principal were very angry indeed and caused quite a bit of distortion in her ability to understand her staff member's behavior. The principal might have done better if she had worked through her feelings before she spoke; if she had used questions to learn exactly what I had been up to and why. Then she would have learned that I was a new teacher, who was merely searching for guidance from the older, more experienced teachers. How could this supervisor have worked through her feelings before she spoke to me? Here are some simple ways she might have verbalized them to her supervisor or to a friend: (1) She could have asked herself how she felt about this young man and his work in the school, using words which clearly labelled her feelings of desertion and betrayal; (2) She could have related her feelings to other situations when she felt let down by a friend, thus helping her to see how strong her feelings were at the moment; or (3) She could have stated what she would like to do to the young man, conveying the angry aggressiveness of her attitudes, by a statement such as, "I'm going to wring your neck." To assure accuracy in the transmission of her feelings during the encounter, the supervisor could have begun each statement with a pronoun followed by a noun which clearly labeled her emotions. "I hate you," or "My anger is rising," or "I feel like firing you," or "How could you be so ungrateful?" are all personal statements that make it clear to the other how one feels.

To repeat, these skills are essential to relationship building, and they would have helped this principal to be more conscious in her dealings with the staff member. There cannot be closeness, friendship, and honesty when individuals cannot clearly communicate their feelings and intentions, and their affection and support.

The clear expression of feelings by a supervisor encourages staff to listen attentively and to become more aware of their supervisor's emotions and frame of reference. It also helps staff acquire their own skills in feeling expression, thus allowing them to establish closer ties with other staff and students. It increases the amount of reliable information supervisors can use as they try to understand the people with whom they work.

When someone speaks to us of her feelings, it is easy to misunderstand. When she sends verbal or non-verbal messages, it is easy to confuse our own feelings with those she is trying to convey. Stereotypes, suppositions, fears, and desires distort the listener's ability to perceive and understand the sender's intentions, as the role play between the principal and her "union organizing" teacher showed. Many supervisors are unaware of these confusions, therefore, improving skills in this area can be difficult.

One way to improve the ability to hear and understand is to use the listening skills discussed in this chapter. Monitoring another's statements in these ways, the receiver can make tentative assumptions about what is being said to her. "Do you mean . . . ?" or "You are saying . . ." or "Do you feel . . ." are three types of responses which can be used to clarify what is being said. Such comments can be effective if they are non-judgmental in tone, and if they show the other her feelings will not be rejected or used against her in some way.

NOTES

1. R. R. Carkhuff, *The Art of Helping* (Amherst, Mass.: Human Resource Development Press, 1987), pp. 1–5; H. B. Karp, *The Change Leader: Using a Gestalt Approach with Work Groups* (San Francisco: Pfeiffer, 1996); Jack Gibb, "The TORI System of Leadership," in J. Pfeiffer and J. Jones (eds.), *The 1972 Annual Handbook for Group Facilitators* (Iowa City: University Associates Press, 1972), pp. 157–162.

2. R. Schwarz, *The Skilled Facilitator: Practical Wisdom for Developing Effective Groups* (San Francisco: Pfeiffer, 1996), pp. 5–14; David Johnson, *Reaching Out: Interpersonal Effectiveness and Self-Actualization* (Englewood Cliffs, N.J.: Prentice-Hall, 1981), pp. 15–46; See also "Five Components Contributing to Effective Interpersonal Communication," in *The 1974 Annual Handbook for Group Facilitators* (La Jolla, Calif.: University Associates Press, 1974), pp. 125–129; S. Jouard, *Self-Disclosure* (New York: Wiley Interscience, 1971); Gerard Egan, *The Skilled Helper: A Systematic Approach to Effective Helping* (Pacific Grove, Calif.: Brooks/Cole Publishing Company, 1990), pp. 56–59.

3. W. H. Cormier and L. S. Cormier, *Interviewing Strategies for Helpers: Fundamental Skills and Cognitive Behavioral Interventions* (Pacific Grove, Calif.: Brooks/Cole Publishing Company, 1985); Stanley W. Rothstein, "Conflict Resolution in a Supportive Environment," *Education and Urban Society*, Vol. VII, No. 2 (February 1975), pp. 193–

206; Johnson, *Reaching Out*; Jack Gibb, "Dynamics Of Leadership and Communication," in *Leadership and Social Change* (Iowa City: University Associates Press, 1971), pp. 85–105.

4. J. Lacan, *Speech and Language in Psychoanalysis*, trans. Anthony Wilden (Baltimore: Johns Hopkins University Press, 1989), pp. 24–26; E. Kris, "The Recovery of Childhood Memories in Psychoanalysis," in *The Psycho-Analytic Study of the Child* (New York: International Universities Press, 1956), pp. 54–58.

5. J. Lacan, *The Seminar of Jacques Lacan*, ed. Jacques Alain Miller, trans. Sylvana Tomaselli (New York: W. W. Norton, 1991), pp. 122–125; Heinz Hartmann, *Essays in Ego Psychology* (New York: International Universities Press, 1964).

6. Elisabeth Roudinesco, *Jacques Lacan & Co.: A History of Psychoanalysis in France, 1925–1985* (Chicago: University of Chicago Press, 1986); Hartmann, *Essays in Ego Psychology*, in which the theory of neutralization is discussed; Egan, *The Skilled Helper*, pp. 29–30; C. R. Rogers, "Reflections on Feelings," *Person Centered Review*, No. 2 (1986), pp. 375–377.

7. T. Anastasi, *Face to Face Communication* (Cambridge, Mass.: Management Center for Cambridge, 1967); R. Carkhuff, *The Art of Helping* (Amherst, Mass.: Human Resource Development Press, 1987); V. Satir, *Peoplemaking* (Palo Alto, Calif.: Science and Behavior Books, 1972); Julia T. Wood, *Relational Communication* (Belmont, Calif.: Wadsworth Publishing Company, 1995), pp. 125–148; Stanley W. Rothstein, *Identity and Ideology: Socio-Cultural Theories of Schooling* (Westport, Conn.: Greenwood Press, 1991), ch. 6; Chris Argyris, "Interpersonal Barriers to Decision-Making," *Harvard Business Review*, No. 44 (1966), pp. 84–97.

8. Basil Bernstein, *The Structuring of Pedagogic Discourse*, Vol. IV, *Class, Codes and Control* (London: Routledge and Kegan Paul, 1990); Stanley W. Rothstein, "The Focus Interview," *The Guidance Clinic* (December 1981), pp. 1–15.

9. Stanley W. Rothstein, *The Voice of the Other: Language as Illusion in the Formation of the Self* (Westport, Conn.: Praeger Publishers, 1993), pp. 10–11; Stanley W. Rothstein, *Schools and Society: New Perspectives in American Education* (Englewood Cliffs, N.J.: Prentice-Hall, 1996), ch. 1.

10. W. J. Rothwell, R. Sullivan, and G. N. McLean, *Practicing Organizational Development: A Guide for Consultants* (San Francisco: Pfeiffer, 1996), pp. 44–47; P. Schmuck et al., *Handbook of Organizational Development* (Palo Alto, Calif.: Mayfield Publishing, 1972), pp. 39–42; also D. Johnson and M. Noonan, "The Effects of Acceptance and Reciprocation of Self-Disclosures on the Development of Trust," *Journal of Counseling Psychology*, Vol. 19 (1972), pp. 411–416; Arthur W. Combs, Donald L. Avila, and William W. Purkey, *Helping Relationships: Basic Concepts for the Helping Professions* (Boston: Allyn and Bacon, 1971).

11. R. Wynn and C. Guditus, *Team Management: Leadership by Consensus* (Columbus, Ohio: Charles E. Merrill Publishing Company, 1984), pp. 72–91; Jack Gibb, "Climate for Trust Formation," in L. Bradford, Jack Gibb, and K. Benne, *T-Group Theory and the Laboratory Method* (New York: John Wiley and Sons, 1964).

12. L. Bradford (ed.), *Group Development* (La Jolla, Calif.: University Associates Press, 1974), pp. 81–89; Jacqueline Jordan Irvine, "Teacher Perspectives: Why Do African-American, Hispanic, and Vietnamese Students Fail?" in Stanley W. Rothstein (ed.), *Handbook of Schooling in Urban America* (Westport, Conn.: Greenwood Press, 1993); D. Kinlaw, *Listening and Communicating Skills* (San Diego, Calif.: University Associates

Press, 1982); F. Walsh, "Conceptualization of Normal Family Processes," in F. Walsh (ed.), *Normal Family Processes* (New York: Guilford, 1993), pp. 3–69.

13. G. Egan, *Change Agent Skills in Helping and Human-Service Settings* (Pacific Grove, Calif.: Brooks/Cole Publishing Company, 1985); M. L. Knapp, *Nonverbal Communication in Human Interaction* (New York: Holt, Rinehart and Winston, 1978), pp. 45–54; Wynn and Guditus, *Team Management*, pp. 83–92.

14. G. J. Neimeyer and P. G. Banikiotes, "Self-Disclosure Flexibility, Empathy, and Perceptions of Adjustment and Attraction," *Journal of Counseling Psychology*, Vol. 28 (1981), pp. 272–275; A. Blumensteil, *Acquaintance: Structural and Relational Features of Laboratory Training* (Doctoral Dissertation, Ann Arbor, Mich.: University Microfilms International, 1968), pp. 95–101; Georg Simmel, *The Sociology of Georg Simmel*, trans. K. Wolff, (Glencoe, Ill.: Free Press, 1950), pp. 126–127.

15. T. Pyszczynski and J. Greenberg, "Self-Regulatory Perseveration and Their Depressive Self-Focusing Style: A Self-Awareness Theory of Depression," *Psychological Bulletin*, Vol. 102 (1987), pp. 122–138; Johnson, *Reaching Out*, pp. 96–97.

16. J. Rappaport, "In Praise of Paradox: A Social Policy of Empowerment over Prevention," *American Journal of Community Psychology*, No. 9 (1981), pp. 1–26; Bradford, *Group Development*, pp. 81–89.

17. G. Yukl, *Leadership in Organizations* (Englewood Cliffs, N.J.: Prentice-Hall, 1989), pp. 124–126; Jack Gibb, "Climate for Trust Formation," in L. Bradford, J. Gibb, and K. Benne, *T-Group Theory and the Laboratory Method* (New York: John Wiley and Sons, 1964), pp. 279–310.

18. Stanley W. Rothstein, "Building and Maintaining High Trust Climates: Training the New Administrator in Feeling Expression and Inquiry Skills," *Education and Urban Society* (November 1976), pp. 81–101.

19. G. Simmel, *Conflict and the Web of Group Affiliations* (Glencoe, Ill.: Free Press, 1955).

20. G. Egan, *The Skilled Helper: A Systematic Approach to Effective Helping* (Pacific Grove, Calif.: Brooks/Cole Publishing Company, 1990), pp. 126–128; G. Blanck and R. Blanck, *Ego Psychology: Theory and Practice* (New York: Columbia University Press, 1974).

21. Stanley W. Rothstein, "Orientations: First Impressions in an Urban Junior High School," *Urban Education*, Vol. 14, No. 1 (April 1979), pp. 91–116.

22. Heinz Hartmann, "Notes on a Theory of Sublimation," *The Psychoanalytic Study of the Child* (New York: International Universities Press, 1955), pp. 9–27.

23. Stanley W. Rothstein, *Schooling the Poor: A Social Inquiry into the American Educational Experience* (Westport, Conn.: Bergin & Garvey, 1994).

24. M. D. Robinson, *Meaningful Counseling* (New York: Human Sciences Press, 1988), ch. 1; A. Blumensteil, unpublished dissertation, pp. 133–140.

25. From my field notes.

26. D. W. Johnson and M. Noonan, "The Effects of Acceptance and Reciprocation of Self-Disclosures on the Development of Trust," *Journal of Counseling Psychology*, No. 19 (1972), pp. 411–416.

5

Psychological Insights: New Tools for School Leaders

QUESTIONS TO THINK ABOUT

1. What is the human ego?
2. What role does it play in the everyday behavior of teachers and students?
3. Why is verbalization an important part of administrative support systems for teachers?
4. What is meant by the process of neutralization?
5. What problems can administrators and teachers face during their first days on the job?
6. What organizational characteristics of modern schools inhibit communication between teachers and supervisors?
7. What is traumatic handling and how does it show itself in schools?

What do school leaders need to know about the ways in which teachers interact with students? First, they should know that these relationships are often determined by whether they are dominated by fear or trust.[1] Second, they should know that administrative support systems are meaningless unless they are based upon a knowledge of the human ego and unless they provide for constant ego support.[2] Finally, setting up a formal communication system within the school organization is crucial if supervisors are to learn what is really happening in classrooms. Weekly individual and group conferences need to be an integral part of any attempt to train reflective teachers. It is only through regularly scheduled meetings that ongoing associations between supervisors, teachers, and students can become the basis for any administrative support system.

For the helping process to take hold, school climates need to be both psychologically and educationally sound. Supportive environments assure teachers and students that they will be heard, that, within the school building, they will

be treated with compassion and empathy. Traumatic handling needs to be eliminated as quickly as possible. Such acts as humiliating, regimenting, physically
punishing, or shaming teachers or students should no longer be tolerated. The
work of teachers and students should not be rejected or compared unfavorably
to that of others. Sarcasm is unacceptable in a school with effective staff development and pedagogy.[3]

Teachers need to learn to communicate better with their students so they can
be more successful in their classwork. They need to use more reflective methods
of instruction and evaluation so that children receive a more relevant and vibrant
classroom experience. Everyone in the school organization needs someone
whom they can talk to about their work and the problems that develop from
week to week. Teachers need to understand that, according to the research literature, withholding positive regard from students because they do not ''deserve'' it is counterproductive. Finally, staff members need to be taught to deal
with their feelings of guilt, anxiety, fear, and depression as they affect their
relations with students.

Conferencing is important because overt behavior is often misunderstood.
What children are trying to say when they behave in angry or disruptive ways
is seldom probed by teachers reflectively. All too often, teachers seem more
interested in getting students to follow the rules, routines, and regulations of the
organization. In such situations, feelings may become confused or repressed,
making it still more difficult for educators to know what students are really
feeling in their classrooms. Supervisory conferences can help teachers become
more aware of their own impulsive actions and the ways in which children
respond to them. They can help teachers learn to use Ego Psychology theory to
help youngsters develop the inner controls they need to do sustained work. And
they can help teachers use problem solving methods that place children at the
center of their own problem identification-resolution cycle.[4]

To use these supervisory methods, which are described in more detail in the
next chapter, staff and administrators have to know something about human
personality, and particularly the human ego. One way of understanding human
behavior is by thinking of human personality in terms of two variables: the
impulsive system and the control structure, or ego.[5] An earlier chapter explained
that the impulsive system is the part of the human personality that harbors the
needs, drives, emotions, and impulses of human beings. It is loosely controlled
by the ego, which has many functions that help individuals select between competing forms of social behavior.

INITIAL PROBLEMS

School leaders need to be aware that new staff go through various learning
experiences, or phases, once they become part of the organization; they develop
ways of doing their work that are peculiarly their own. This happens the instant
a new teacher enters the school and begins to play out her new role inside the

building. In the movement from being a newcomer to someone who will be, in time, a veteran, the teacher's control structure, or ego, undergoes a series of shocks and strains as it tries to deal with the problems she encounters inside the school. Studies of the transitional period from college student to teacher have identified some of its difficulties. Exactly what happens to a particular individual cannot be predicted with accuracy. But certain problems need to be anticipated if the newcomer is to succeed. All staff and students deserve psychological and educational support. They are all going through socialization processes that are transforming them from what they have been to what they will be once the schoolwork begins. New staff are moving away from their student identities toward those of the professional educator; children are in the long and arduous process of going through the grade system so they can become adults. The control structure, or ego, of both groups is deeply involved in these socializing and learning experiences. Their cognition functions in particular need to be strengthened if they are to perceive and understand school life accurately. What can skillful supervisors do to help their egos perform this important task for staff members and students? How can they help teachers and students to be in contact with one another and with their own thoughts and feelings? What does a skillful supervisor need to do to keep his new teachers on an even keel during their first stressful days on the job?

Researchers have found that administrative support efforts must be employed within the total school setting.[6] This requires weekly individual and group meetings. The "how-to" of educational support takes place in these conferences where teachers are encouraged to express their thoughts and focus on their feelings and actions inside the school. In these conferences, staff members are encouraged to reflect upon the educational and emotional relationships that are developing in their classrooms and to identify and resolve ongoing problems. The support system or ego of individual teachers is strengthened in these meetings. Staff members become more aware of what is really happening in their interactions with others, and their control functions are constantly flexed and strengthened by these reflective sessions.

Why is it important to hold weekly meetings? For one reason, if a teacher dislikes a child, she may not always be aware of these feelings or how deep they are. Staff members like to think they treat all their students the same, that they like them all. But until the teacher has an opportunity to discuss her feelings, she may not be fully aware of how her behavior is provoking the children. She may not be aware of the double messages she is sending to students or the reasons for her behavior.

How does a supervisor know what to talk about at staff meetings? She can use several approaches. She can listen to the teacher and then respond to the teacher's comments about other staff or students. She can ask the teacher what she knows about each child in her classroom. Why does she know so much about some children and so little about others? How can she explain knowing so little about Juan Alvarez, for example? Are the children she knows little about outsiders in her classroom? And if they are, what is she doing to help them make friends? What is she doing to integrate them into classroom life? Too often, teachers do not accept children because they are doing poorly in class or appear to be shy and timid. These very same children are probably also not being accepted in the yard or at lunch. Other children are not playing with them, and they are eating alone. Teachers often fail to notice such things, and, too often, they fail to support these newcomers adequately.

The formal scheduling of weekly supervisory meetings provides an environment in which ego support and personality strengthening can take place. Teachers can talk about, and reflect upon, their classroom experiences. But these conferences require school supervisors to become more skilled and knowledgable so they can help teachers develop greater awareness of their actions and those of others inside the school building.

EGO FUNCTIONS

Ego Psychology had a mixed reputation until Anna Freud's works were published.[7] It is only in the last few decades that a literature and technology has developed based on Ego Psychology theory and its use in improving interpersonal relations at home and in the workplace. Sigmund Freud, Heinz Hartmann, Fritz Redl, and David Wineman were among the leaders in the development of this theory, which advocates the practical use of ego support in the helping method.[8]

From the theory and research associated with this group of scholars, we can infer that the ego is a part of the human psyche and has a number of important functions.[9] The ego helps people understand the world outside of themselves. The ego makes assumptions about what things are like and warns when there is danger. It estimates and calculates possibilities and consequences. I won't report to the dean's office, a boy says to himself impulsively, remembering what he has heard or experienced there. His ego, if it is intact, may then interject itself: It isn't good to be late. Remember what the dean does to boys who don't report directly to his office.

The ego also summarizes the social situation of teachers: the influence and primary groups they belong to, as well as the rules and regulations of the school. When a person's urges and impulses threaten to conflict with the social norms and mores of the organization, the ego provides warning signals about the potential results if such impulses were transformed into behavior. The ego assesses the school world in which teachers must do their work, and it warns them of potential danger and unpleasantness when their impulsive urges threaten to come into conflict with the realities of the school organization. The ego discovers and evaluates what is happening in the outside world, suggesting responses that will be most suitable to different situations.

Another important function of the ego is to discover what is happening within the mind or impulsive system of the individual supervisor, teacher, or student. Some contents of the impulsive system are not known to the control structure because they represent repressed emotions or are embedded in the unconscious. If the ego does not know about them, however, it cannot exercise its control function. Therefore, the ego is continually engaged in searching out and monitoring feelings, urges, drives, anxieties, and fears that cause individuals to behave in particular ways when they are unaware of their impulsive strivings.

Self-insight, then, is an important function of the control structure, or ego. It is also the task of the ego to become aware of the values that motivate the individual's behavior. Certain actions would not be accepted by a person's conscience or superego because of deep-seated beliefs about what is right or wrong, fair or unfair. But researchers have discovered that such values can also be unconscious and, therefore, outside the knowledge and control of the ego.[10] In such cases, the ego must ferret out these attitudes. The school administrator's job is to become self-aware so she can help the staff person's ego begin the process of cognition, and so she can help her face anxieties and guilt.

To the regulatory functions of the ego and superego can be added those of identity formation and self-esteem. In these control structures, impulsive energies can be balanced and neutralized so they are in greater harmony with the individual's social world. Self-esteem, or self-acceptance, determines how well a person can handle stress and crises, and how clearly she can see, hear, and understand others. People with low self-esteem have had experiences that portrayed them as unworthy or incompetent. Such people may come to see themselves as deformed or abnormal. They may doubt their abilities and intelligence and look to others for guidance and support; or they may feel that all relationships will end unhappily, once others come to know them well. This explains why some individuals distance themselves from others to guard against further rejection. Such behavior introduces many distortions into the communication process.[11]

A person's self-esteem remains relatively constant; her feelings about herself remain the same over time and in most situations. This means that these feelings are important in relationship building and in understanding the communications of others. It also means that high self-esteem and acceptance is significant for administrators who want to hear and understand what others are saying to them. A surprising number of supervisors, though, tend to think and act cynically. Such attitudes and behavior undercut any effort a leader may undertake to develop supervisory support systems. A supervisor's health and psychological well-being depend, to a large degree, on the feelings she has about herself. If she sees herself as unworthy or incompetent, her perceptions will be influenced by these feelings. Is she respected and well-liked? Do staff see her as a helpful and capable person? These questions cannot be answered accurately by school administrators who have isolated themselves; they can only be answered with certainty when the supervisor has friendly and open relationships with the staff members she serves.

Relevant research confirms what everyone knows: persons with high self-esteem tend to be more optimistic and friendly; they are more accepting of themselves and others with whom they work.[12] Conversely, persons with low self-esteem tend to be more anxious, depressed, cynical, and insecure about themselves and their relationships with others.

Another function of the control structure is to coordinate and balance human behavior. The ego often determines whether the demands of the impulsive system will be met or not: whether the requirements of the outside world, or of conscience, will dictate how an individual acts in certain situations. For instance, if the conscience of a school administrator becomes the driving force behind her actions, she may feel that the "right thing" is being done even when her behavior hurts others or denies some of the demands of her own impulsive system. But if she yields to her impulses, she may find herself coming into conflict with others who are offended by her conscienceless behavior. The ego, or control structure, tries to keep a balance between these internal demands and the demands of the school world.

A healthy ego seeks not only to know what is happening inside itself and in the surrounding world, but also makes choices about what sorts of behavior make the most sense in particular situations. Since there are many ways to respond to situations, the ego has a choice. This choice is not based solely upon whether an individual can pay the "price" for her behavior, as we can see from the following example. Assume that an assistant principal in an urban junior high school decides his principal's treatment of other administrators is unprofessional and sarcastic, but he keeps silent because he is afraid to draw the anger of his superior. Of course he has a number of ways he can react to this situation. He can deny that the treatment really did humiliate the other supervisors. He can point to their lack of response and characterize it as proof they were not really injured. In this case, he will be annoyed with himself and anyone else who suggests that the principal's behavior was offensive and that someone should have said something. He may, as another response, simply withdraw and say little at subsequent supervisory meetings. He may decide that the others "had it coming to them" and avoid these fellow supervisors whenever possible; he may sit as far away from them as he can at subsequent meetings. Alternatively, he may decide to leave the school entirely, quietly asking for a transfer. If the assistant principal decides to be proactive, he could bring the principal's actions to the attention of the district office, accusing him of improper conduct. If he does nothing, he will have to live with feelings of inadequacy, guilt, anxiety, and humiliation.

This assistant principal has still more choices he can make. He could ask the principal if he is aware of his behavior, or he could ask an administrator who is closer to the chief to do this chore. He could ask others for suggestions. His ego will have many choices to make.

DYSFUNCTIONS

An inability to control libidinal or impulsive energies appears to be linked to poor interpersonal relationships.[13] In the school, such attitudes can be characterized by an "I don't care," or "I don't need anyone" attitude. For example, an insecure staff member may be unable to enter into a relationship with other teachers or students. Administrative support systems do not deal with the past experiences and maladaptations that caused this behavior; such work is best done by a therapist. Rather, administrators should focus on how these ways of responding to others are affecting the teacher now. They should try to help teachers become more reflective and aware of their patterns of behavior in the school building: "You always get mad first and think afterward!" Skillful supervisors can ask such teachers whether such adjustments, which may have worked in the past, are still fulfilling their old functions and providing them with the same satisfactions.

Teachers whose typical mode of behavior is one of anger may respond in the school by projecting their feelings onto others. This behavior is often related to feelings that they are being evaluated poorly by supervisors and other staff persons. In these circumstances, supervisors should subordinate value judgments and criticisms to establish a good relationship; they should gently confront such persons about the validity of their perceptions and understandings. A special problem that haunts many school administrators (and teachers) is that of the paranoid slant. This pattern of thought (and behavior) is rooted in the feeling of supervisors that they cannot make a difference and that knowledge of their ineffectiveness is widely shared by others in the school. When supervisors adopt the paranoid slant, they find it necessary to shift the blame or guilt they feel (for being inadequate) to others with whom they work ("If you people did your job, things wouldn't be so screwed up around here"). Feelings of ineffectiveness ("I guess I'm just a born loser") cause administrators and teachers to be careful in their associations in fear that other people might discover or confirm in their own minds evidence of the supervisor's inferiority or inadequacy. People with a paranoid slant are afraid that if they are open and honest, others will learn of their inadequacies and use this knowledge against them. This feeling that others are plotting against them makes it more difficult for such supervisors (or teachers) to speak openly and has the unintended effect of moving people away from them.

The tensions of the paranoid slant lead to an insight that, when problems occur, others should be blamed. In their own minds, staff members with a paranoid slant become the victim, not of their own inadequacies but of the plotting and inefficiency of others. In this way, the guilt that they felt initially (perhaps unconsciously) is no longer theirs. It has been transferred to those with whom they work. Administrators and teachers find it more difficult to know what is happening around them in this state of mind. They often repeat behaviors that cause others to become unfriendly and hostile, thus fulfilling the assumptions of the paranoid slant. Educators with a paranoid slant have little insight about their own behavior (transferring blame to, and provoking others) or motivations (reacting to their own fears and misconceptions). They find themselves unable to admit mistakes and errors (That would be giving them the ammunition they need!).

The breakdown of communication channels in schools, and the strain such failures cause in everyone, often lead to an improper ego development in supervisors and teachers. Poor communication can cause ego regression, in which teachers (and students) lose skills, abilities, and understandings they have already mastered. This can happen when staff are initiated into an authoritarian climate that deemphasizes people skills and problem solving methods.

Another related form of defensive behavior is transference, which refers to the displacement of impulsive energies from one person to another.[14] Usually the shift is from one's attitudes toward parents or early authority figures to individuals in the present. Thus staff may show warmth and affection toward school administrators when they first meet them. But after a period of time, other, more puzzling, behaviors may become evident. These behaviors are also associated with the kinds of relationships teachers or students had with their parents. Therefore staff may unknowingly use this transference phenomenon so they can react to new authority persons in ways which were comfortable for them in the past. They reactivate old attitudes and ways of responding so they feel less anxious and apprehensive. They want to act toward the new leader as they did toward other powerful people in their past. Researchers have defined transference as a syndrome that is energized by a compulsion to repeat the feelings and attitudes that belonged to past relationships onto present-day relations. They interpret ongoing experiences with others in terms of their past associations. Greenacre, an important investigator, dealt with transference by focusing on the mother-child dyad, which she felt contained the core of the transference phenomenon. The attitude of the child toward her mother was developed in a relationship wherein the child was essentially powerless and dependent for many years. The transference of these feelings onto administrators (or teachers) can release much unneutralized aggression and drive energy; it can cause distortion in the reception and understanding of communications between people working together in the school.[15]

When supervisors try to use communication channels to change the way staff react to them, they usually encounter resistances. These resistances are the typical ways staff members respond to such efforts, and they are deeply rooted in the staff member's self-concepts and identities. Staff defend themselves against efforts to change them because this supervisory behavior sends them a hidden message: You are not okay the way you are. Otherwise, there would be no reason to try to change you. Defensiveness causes staff to look away from their behavior and ways of doing things. Teachers want to go on acting as they have acted in the past, especially if such behaviors have served them well in the past. If they were friendly toward those who had power over them, they want to retain that way of reacting to present-day authority persons in their life. If they were angry or hostile, they often have an interest and deep-seated reason for wishing to remain that way. Administrators have difficult tasks: (1) to deal with transference and resistance by accepting the staff member's stage of development; and (2) to move her slowly from a lack of awareness of impulsive behavior toward greater insight and control over these features of her personality. There can be no change in the relationships between supervisors and teachers as long as these types of problems remain unresolved.

EGO SUPPORT

Ego support is an important tool for school administrators.[16] It requires more than merely encouraging or complimenting a staff member in a general way by saying, "That was very good," or "You are very nice." These remarks are nothing more than flattery and mean little in a clinical, scientific sense. They make staff feel good for the moment, but they also establish feelings of anxiety and dependence upon the authority figure. (Will she feel that the next thing the teacher does is equally as good? Or will she disapprove?)

Anxiety and poor self-concepts cannot be affected by such compliments. The self-identities of teachers have been learned and internalized at an early age in primary relationships with parents and significant others; they were also affected by their successes and failures in social and intellectual activities. Generalized compliments have little lasting effect upon persons who have a poor sense of themselves as individuals and educators. Even the best teacher lives in a society in which most believe that "those who can, do; those who can't, teach." Teachers need more specific support if they are to properly appreciate their growth and development as professional persons. Only with such support can they become aware of their own areas of increasing strength and competency and use these new insights in their daily work with students. Initiative and a spirit of inquiry are fostered when ego functions are strengthened in this way. The courage to disagree and to try new things is another outcome of such supervisory practices.

Unfortunately, there is little psychological support for the human ego in today's schools. Rather, there is a great deal of anxiety and defensiveness between supervisors, teachers, and students.[17] Teachers often see school administrators as untrustworthy and overly judgmental; administrators all too often assume that teachers are lazy, apathetic, and mercenary. Teachers believe they must submit to the directive leadership of incompetent supervisory personnel; administrators frequently talk about the disloyalty and pedagogical errors of teachers. The relations between supervisors and teachers must be improved. One way to improve them is to establish greater empathy and regard between the two groups by strengthening the individual control structures (or egos) of both staff members and supervisors. This can best be done by encouraging supervisors and teachers to verbalize their thoughts and feelings in regular supervisory meetings.

Many teachers are quiet and introspective because they fear ridicule or rejection. Some use this way of responding because they unconsciously want the supervisor to understand them without words, as their parents did when they were infants. Of course, this is impossible. School administrators need to move toward these quiet ones; they need to learn about them; and they need to encourage them to explain themselves and their behavior in words. This can only be done in an atmosphere of mutual self-disclosure. The relationships that develop between them are an important ego-building technique in themselves. When teachers verbalize their feelings and classroom experiences to the supervisor, they set in motion a process that greatly strengthens the functioning of their control structures or egos.[18] Verbalization forces teachers to substitute symbols for their vaguely remembered experiences; it makes them declare openly their intentions and reveals the way in which they see the school and classroom within which they work. Verbalization helps staff members to develop inner controls by assisting their control structure, or ego, so it can neutralize impulses and emotions emanating from the impulsive system. Some researchers have found that verbalization and neutralization help individuals understand and tolerate frustration better in their work and everyday lives.[19]

Ego-building is best done by encouraging teachers (and students) to describe and interpret their feelings and experiences about ongoing classroom experiences. Everyone has complete consciousness; they know everything that is happening to them. Often, however, the conscious knowledge is buried in the preconscious or unconscious mind. Therefore it is best never to *tell* someone something you want them to know. They already know it. They can usually tell you about it once you have established a trusting and friendly relationship with them. Then, with help, they can draw the necessary conclusions from such information. At such moments, questions such as What does that mean to you? or How would you interpret that? can help teachers synthesize and evaluate their own feelings and behavior. Advice giving, which is so common in today's schools, should be avoided whenever possible: it tends to intimidate staff members, making them overly dependent upon the evaluation and good will of supervisors.

Verbalization within the framework of a friendly, trusting association is the key. In such settings, the neutralization and heightened awareness of the teacher can grow to fruition. In trusting relationships teachers develop greater awareness and sensitivity to their own behavior and that of their students. Neutralization in supervisory meetings is strengthened by verbalization, which helps teachers understand and cope with actions and emotions in the classroom. The positive climate of conferences is important because it provides participants with feelings of trust and mutual regard that are essential to the helping process. The administrator establishes a comfortable, accepting environment that is built up over time. Once the teacher is convinced of the supervisor's reliability, she is more likely to begin expressing herself openly, finding satisfaction in the process that helps her to identify and resolve classroom problems.

Record #1

Today I met with a special education teacher. He was nervous and upset as he sat in front of me. His hands moved constantly and his facial muscles were very tight. This surprised me, since I assumed we were friends. Finally he began to speak about his problem: one of the teachers in his department was an alcoholic. This teacher was doing a poor job and hurting the children he was supposed to be serving. Something had to be done to protect the children. The other staff and secretaries wanted this special education teacher to be their spokesman; they wanted him to lead in an effort to get this man dismissed. But this young man wanted no part in such an action. He did not want to be pushed into such a leadership role.

We talked for quite a while. He admitted he didn't like this alcoholic teacher. In fact, he remembered an incident in which this man had humiliated him in front of others. It happened soon after the young man was appointed to the school. The alcoholic teacher accused him of being a weak, ineffective teacher who was causing problems for the rest of the staff. This teacher remembered his feelings at the time this happened: he felt a surge of hatred toward his tormentor.

Then this teacher had an insight. He had sworn that he would get even with this alcoholic man but then put such thoughts out of his mind. Subconsciously, he plotted against the man, talking to others about his drinking and poor behavior in class. He wasn't being pushed to lead in the effort to get rid of this man. He was the leader!

This revelation startled both of us. The teacher was surprised at his own deviousness and the strength of his first unconscious feelings. He decided, then and there, to write a plan to redress the damage he had done to this teacher. He had no desire to harm him further and felt that he had to go out of his way to make amends.

This was an instance where unconscious impulses and feelings distorted the perceptions of a teacher and caused behavior he was unaware of until he verbalized his feelings and actions in this reflective session.[20]

Open communication and ego support require that the work of identifying and resolving classroom or school problems be done by the teacher. The skillful supervisor must not help the teacher do things they can do for themselves. The supervisory conference, which is covered in Chapter 6, encourages the teacher to focus on her problems. What are they? Who is involved in them? How is she responding to the feelings and behavior of others? These questions ask staff to become more aware of others and more skillful in identifying and resolving classroom problems. They ask teachers to strengthen and use their own interpretive skills. This helps the teachers see, understand, and respond consciously to the school world they work in.

Verbalizing feelings acts as a substitute for actions that might hurt the teacher in her relationships with supervisors, parents, and students. It postpones overt behavior and causes the staff person to think about aspects of the situation that may have escaped her attention in the past. As individuals learn to transfer libidinal energies from the emotional to the more rational mode through the verbalization of feelings, they are better able to place these emotions under the control of the ego. The ego, in turn, becomes further strengthened and better able to rationalize the interactions that take place with others. If supervisors cannot talk to staff in this way, they cannot learn the information necessary to understand what is really happening in the school. They cannot act in conscious, rational ways, or know how they are being understood and perceived by those with whom they work. They cannot know where their teachers are in their personal and professional development, and they cannot provide them with meaningful supervision.

Moreover, when a staff member cannot express herself openly, or when she is unaware of her feelings, she experiences anxiety, frustration, and discomfort. These feelings, which are often related to past events, build up and force her to seek some way of relieving her growing inner tensions. If she does not express these feelings, or if she denies them, they tend to reappear at odd times in irrational and undesired ways. If administrators and teachers do not deal with these feelings as they arise, they may have to deal with a whole configuration of them later; and these feelings will seem to be detached from anything that is happening in the present: they will appear as irrational and unreasonable behavior and cause distress to others. A staff person may prevent herself from understanding her impulses for a while, but the patterns of behavior that she builds on these unconscious attitudes will keep slipping out in her gestures, speech, voice, and relationships with others. Such non-verbal communications are caused by a person's inability to relate to her inner feelings and impulses and to those of others, and by her general lack of sensitivity to the emotional relationships she is forming inside the school.[21]

People have the capacity to like and dislike one another.[22] This makes it possible for them to associate and to carry on social intercourse. They often feel ambivalence in their needs and intentions, their ability to accept and reject features for people or situations. It is not known why people have these negative and positive reactions; it is only known that the reactions are related to the need for love and acceptance. These same needs force people to hide their angry emotions, their feelings of hostility and negativeness. But the suppression or repression of feelings causes a new and more complicated emotion to appear: anxiety. Later Freudian thought held that tension and conflict between two psychic structures (the ego and the id, for example) produced anxiety and a need for the ego to institute defensive measures. The cycle—conflict, anxiety, defense—led to compromises between the ego and the id. Together with guilt, anger, and hostility, these symptoms formed a configuration of defensive attitudes that are often seen in schools today, where love and acceptance are often conspicuous by their absence.

Supervisors, too, need someone to talk to about their feelings and behavior. They need someone who can make them more aware of the moments when their anger shows itself in unexpected and undesired ways. They should be able to see when they are upset with others, when they are taking over the work function from staff, when they are demeaning or humiliating teachers or students by acting in angry or provocative ways. Every supervisor and teacher needs to struggle with ambivalent feelings that grow out of their work with others.

If staff do not have supervisors with whom they can talk about their hopes, dreams, fears, and aspirations, they suffer a diminution of spirit and social isolation. If they work in schools where they have no friends, and do not perceive administrators and fellow staff as helpful persons, they suffer from feelings of exclusion and loneliness. If they are not permitted self-direction and a growing sense of achievement, their interest and involvement in their schoolwork decreases. A teacher who has no one to talk to about her work cannot become sensitive to her own needs or the needs of the children she is trying to teach.

FREEDOM FROM TRAUMATIC HANDLING

An encounter between an administrator and staff person can be labelled "traumatic" when it produces disturbed feelings and responses in either one of them.[23] This can happen when an experience reminds either one of them of a past event or forces them to endure an attack on their self-systems. An administrator can cause a teacher or student to experience a traumatic episode when she touches upon matters that inflame past problems or create new ones, and when she evokes anxiety, fear or defensiveness. Whether a staff person will be traumatized by a supervisor's behavior depends upon her previous life and associations, and the nature of her relationship with the school administrator. Teachers are often mistreated because of the reactive nature of school administration. Yet staff have the ability to withstand and overcome some measure of wrong or traumatic handling; many take it in stride and manage to socialize their aggressive, hostile responses. Nevertheless, school administrators should try to make certain, as much as possible, that teachers and students are not humiliated during the school day. Two points should be emphasized:

1. Administrators should avoid angry, unfriendly confrontations that "show up" staff persons in front of others. Under no circumstances should they shame teachers in public, especially in front of students. Releasing angry impulses is not acceptable behavior even if it makes the school administrator "feel better"; threats of any kind must be avoided and the consequences of competition dealt with constructively. Situations that expose staff to ridicule, anxiety, or fear must be eliminated. Favoritism and inconsistent treatment, as well as tactlessness, must also be avoided. These principles apply with greater force to the way teachers handle the defenseless, dependent school children with whom they come in contact.

2. Along with this freedom from traumatic handling in the present, it is necessary for administrators to know something about the previous schooling and life of staff members (and students). It is necessary to know something about any previous traumatic handling they suffered. The behavior of staff toward administration must be understood within the context of past schooling experiences and the feelings they are generating in the present. Aggressive or perverse behavior and impulses may be related to other times, places, and persons. A supervisor's response to the demands of a

teacher that a boy be permanently barred from her class should be based on knowledge of the teacher's previous dealings with disruptive students. Supervisors need to think about past situations in which the staff member was wrongly treated by administration and use this information to design a strategy that does not repeat past mistakes. Therefore supervisors need to possess knowledge and skills in the areas of feeling expression and inquiry, and they need to be aware of the normal responses and development of teachers and students in the school setting.

All staff members and students go through experiences in schools that have some traumatic impact. Everyday school life is impersonal, and mass schools cannot be so insulated and controlled that individuals are always protected from these upsetting experiences. The youngster who has been humiliated in front of his classmates and has to spend the rest of the school year dealing with his feelings of shame and embarrassment has been traumatized. Yet the level of trauma is not as great as that associated with the death of a parent or serious personal injuries. Even so, the trauma of living and working in unfriendly and unsupportive environments can have a severe effect on a teacher's or child's personality and intellectual development. Seldom do teachers, for example, recognize the symptoms of certain kinds of trauma; passivity can actually go unnoticed (or praised) in many schools because the students do not disrupt classroom routines. With competition, the rule that is in effect in most schools today, there are many losers. The grading of deportment and work in a competitive ethos can be viewed as an example of the traumatic handling of children, especially when it happens in kindergarten and grade one.

Record #2

Sara, who had spent four months in a kindergarten in a suburban school, was becoming withdrawn and disinterested in her schoolwork. She told her mother the work was too easy. Her mother asked for more information and was told that Sara was in the "green" ability group in class. When pressed further, Sara said that was the smart group and that another group, the "brownies" as they were called, were for the "dummies." Here was an example of tracking children in kindergarten!

When Sara's mother spoke to the teacher, she confirmed what Sara had told her. The children in the brown group were mostly from a nearby military base and much slower than neighborhood children. "Do you know," this teacher said, "those children don't even know their colors! They don't know their numbers! Why many of them don't even know they have a last name!"

The injuriousness to the self-concepts of children in this situation is self-evident, but the teacher seemed to be completely unaware of it. Unsupportive, cold contact with teachers who feel the children are incompetent and unworthy persons certainly causes trauma in school children. For the trauma is inherent in the treatment of these "dummies" by teachers and by other children in the class.[24]

The commitment to provide administrative support systems for teachers begins with a specific problem: how to restructure the school organization to improve the communication patterns between staff, students, and supervisors. It ends with the development of an ethical and cultural system that is at variance with traditional educational practice today: one that seeks to improve the quality of life for everyone working and learning in the school building.

The benefits of such support systems are many: (1) they help teachers and counselors understand the emotional and behavioral consequences of their actions; (2) they help staff members understand their own behavior and contributions to situations of stress and conflict; (3) they help teachers see that there are many different ways to do their work; (4) they help staff learn how they process information and the distortions they are prone to as a result of their unique social and psychological history; (5) they help teachers and students gain an increased measure of empathy for each other and learn to see the other person's viewpoint; (6) they help staff accept all kinds of behavior as meaningful; (7) they help staff become more flexible in their use of authority so they can limit the frustration and anxiety levels of children; (8) they help staff use inquiry methods to learn about the problems of individual children; and (9) they help staff develop their own ways of identifying and resolving classroom problems.

In these ways the school and its professional staff are made more responsive to their own needs and those of the students they serve. Supervisors ''work through'' their staff members; they do not take over the work and show how it should be done. They assume the role of the facilitator, the inquirer, and the friendly co-professional.

Ego support efforts are basically face-to-face engagements in which the supervisor, because of her training and insight into her own behavior, the behavior of others, and the impact of certain situations on individuals, helps staff members to work in more conscious, effective ways.

SUMMARY

Administrative support systems are needed in today's schools. They provide teachers with moments during the school day when they can think about, or reflect upon, what they are doing in their classrooms. Which of their children do they know well and which are strangers to them? How is their behavior affecting the behavior of the children in their classes? What roles are they playing when a child is an outcast or behaves in disapproved ways? In weekly conferences, teachers can be given an opportunity to identify and resolve ongoing classroom problems before they become unmanageable.

Support systems for teachers need to be based upon the supervisor's knowledge of Ego Psychology. What role does the ego, or control structure, play in the behavior of teachers and students? How can it be used to help teachers use themselves more consciously in their work with students? These methods of support have only one tool at their command: the word. It is only by changing behavior and impulsiveness into language that teachers (and students) can get a better idea about how they are acting in classrooms. Verbalization is the only way to increase their levels of consciousness so they can begin to neutralize and control disruptive and antisocial behaviors. Reflective teachers have an opportunity to develop greater inner controls in themselves and in the students with whom they work.

ACTIVITIES

1. Observe how often a supervisor works one-on-one with teachers. Are the conferences random affairs, occurring only when there are severe problems that need to be attended to? Or are they part of a regular routine? Do teachers speak openly to administrators, or are they guarded in their comments? Does trust dominate relationships? Write down some of your thoughts and be ready to present them to your class.

2. Set up a conferencing schedule with someone you can talk to easily. Talk about what you are doing in your classroom, and why you are doing those things. Then begin to talk more about the feelings that are being generated in your classroom or school. Who is involved in these interactions? Talk about this in some detail. What problems are these people causing you? Tell us more about this. What feelings can you express about them and about your own actions? Make sure you express feelings and not thoughts! What could you do to make things better? Write these ideas down so you can talk about them the next time you meet with any of these people.

NOTES

1. Stanley W. Rothstein, "The Socialization of the School Administrator," *Private School Quarterly* (Spring 1983), pp. 52–60; Richard J. Altenbaugh, "Italian and Mexican Responses to Schooling: Assimilation or Resistance?" in Stanley W. Rothstein (ed.), *Class, Culture and Race in American Schools: A Handbook* (Westport, Conn.: Greenwood Press, 1996), pp. 91–106; Basil Bernstein, *Theoretical Studies towards a Sociology of Language*, Vol. 1, *Class, Codes and Control* (London: Routledge & Kegan Paul, 1975), pp. 12–17; R. A. Spitz, *The First Year of Life* (New York: International Press, 1965), pp. 94–95; E. Kris, "The Recovery of Childhood Memories in Psychoanalysis," in *The Psychoanalytic Study of the Child* (New York: International Universities Press, 1956), p. 76.

2. Larry Cuban, *How Teachers Taught: Constancy and Change in American Classrooms 1890–1980* (New York: Longman, 1984), pp. 22–25; Basil Bernstein, *The Structuring of Pedagogic Discourse*, Vol. IV, *Class, Codes and Control* (London: Routledge and Kegan Paul, 1990); F. Redl and D. Wineman, *Children Who Hate* (New York: Free Press, 1951), pp. 29–44, 195–205; J. Lacan, "The Function of Language in Psychoanalysis," in W. E. Steinkraus (ed.), *The Language of the Self* (Baltimore: John Hopkins, 1968), pp. 39.

3. John Ogbu, *Minority Education and Caste* (New York: Academic Press, 1978), pp. 220–228; F. Redl and D. Wineman, *The Aggressive Child* (Glencoe, Ill.: Free Press, 1957), pp. 58–67, 284–302.

4. Julia T. Wood, *Relational Communication* (Belmont, Calif.: Wadsworth Publish-

ing Company, 1995), pp. 225–250; Stanley W. Rothstein, "The Focus Interview," *The Guidance Clinic* (December 1981), pp. 1–6; G. Blanck and R. Blanck, *Ego Psychology: Theory and Practice* (New York: Columbia University Press, 1974), pp. 53–60.

5. P. A. Eckert, N. Abeles, and R. N. Graham, "Symptom Severity, Psychotherapy Process and Outcome," *Professional Psychology: Research and Practice*, No. 19 (1988), pp. 560–564; Edith Jacobson, *The Self and the Object World* (New York: International Universities Press, 1964); J. Lacan, "The Function of Language in Psychoanalysis," in W. E. Steinkraus (ed.), *The Language of the Self* (Baltimore: John Hopkins, 1968), p. 39.

6. Jacobson, *The Self and the Object World*, pp. 19–21; Wood, *Relational Communication*, pp. 6–17.

7. Heinz Hartmann, *Essays in Ego Psychology* (New York: International Universities Press, 1964), p. 81; Stanley W. Rothstein, "Conflict Resolution in a Supportive Environment," *Education and Urban Society*, (February 1975), pp. 193–199; Jacobson, *The Self and the Object World*, ch. 2.

8. Peter Gay, *Freud: A Life for Our Time* (New York: Doubleday, 1989), pp. 412–414; William G. Thomas, "Experiential Education—A Rationale for Creative Problem Solving," *Education and Urban Society* (February 1975), pp. 172–181; Rothstein, "The Focus Interview," pp. 1–6; G. Blanck and R. Blanck, *Ego Psychology*, pp. 344–346.

9. C. R. Rogers, "Reflections on Feelings" *Person Centered Review*, No. 2 (1986), pp. 375–377; Hartmann, *Essays in Ego Psychology*, p. 145; Jacques Lacan, *Speech and Language in Psychoanalysis*, trans. A. Wilden (Baltimore and London: Johns Hopkins University Press, 1989).

10. C. Surra and R. Milardo, "The Social Psychological Context of Developing Relationships," in W. H. Jones and D. Perlman (eds.), *Advances in Personal Relationships*, Vol. 3 (London: Jessica Kingsley, 1991), pp. 1–36; P. Greenacre, "Certain Technical Problems in the Transference Relationship," *Journal of the American Psychoanalytic Association*, Vol. 7 (1959), pp. 484–502.

11. D. Kinlaw, *Listening and Communicating Skills* (San Diego: University Associates Press, 1982); L. Bradford (ed.), *Group Development* (La Jolla, Calif.: University Associates Press, 1974), pp. 81–89; Redl and Wineman, *Children Who Hate*, pp. 318–393.

12. Jacques Lacan, *The Seminar of Jacques Lacan*, Book II, ed. Jacques-Alain Miller, trans. Sylvana Tomaselli (New York: W. W. Norton, 1991); Jack Gibb, "Climate for Trust Formation," in L. Bradford, Jack Gibb, and K. Benne, *T-Group Theory and the Laboratory Method* (New York: John Wiley and Sons, 1964), pp. 279–310; Stanley W. Rothstein, "Building and Maintaining High Trust Climates: Training the New Administrator in Feeling Expression and Inquiry Skills," *Education and Urban Society* (November 1976), pp. 81–101.

13. Jacobson, *The Self and the Object World*, pp. 61–62; H. Hartmann, "Notes on a Theory of Sublimation," in *The Psychoanalytic Study of the Child* (New York: International Universities Press, 1956), pp. 9–25; Rogers, "Reflections on Feelings," pp. 375–377.

14. Stanley W. Rothstein, *The Voice of the Other: Language as Illusion in the Formation of the Self* (Westport, Conn.: Praeger Publishers, 1993), pp. 1–23; Rothstein, "The Focus Interview."

15. From my field notes.

16. Rothstein, *The Voice of the Other*, pp. 1–13; M. S. Mahler, *On Human Symbiosis*

and the Vicissitudes of Individuation (New York: International Universities Press, 1968), pp. 6–15; Jacobson, *The Self and the Object World*, pp. 60–62.

17. Jacqueline Jordan Irvine, "Teacher Perspectives: Why Do African-American, Hispanic, and Vietnamese Students Fail?" in Stanley W. Rothstein (ed.), *Handbook of Schooling in Urban America* (Westport, Conn.: Greenwood Press, 1993); Redl and Wineman, *Children Who Hate*, pp. 306–310.

18. From my field notes.

19. Harry Stack Sullivan, *The Collected Works of Harry Stack Sullivan*, Vols. I and II (New York: W. W. Norton, 1956), pp. 263–312; Rothstein, "The Focus Interview," pp. 357–360.

20. Stanley W. Rothstein, "Teachers and Students in Urban Schools," in Stanley W. Rothstein (ed.), *Handbook of Schooling in Urban America* (Westport, Conn.: Greenwood Press, 1993), pp. 189–194.

21. F. Redl and D. Wineman, *The Aggressive Child* (Glencoe, Ill.: Free Press, 1957), pp. 58–60.

22. H. Hartmann and R. M. Lowenstein, "Notes on the Superego," in *The Psychoanalytic Study of the Child* (New York: International Universities Press, 1962), pp. 42–81.

23. Redl and Wineman, *The Aggressive Child*, pp. 61–62; Sigmund Freud, *The Ego and the Id*, trans. Joan Riviere (New York: W. W. Norton, 1960), pp. 63–66.

24. Stanley W. Rothstein, "Researching the Power Structure: Personalized Power and Institutionalized Charisma in the Principalship," *Interchange: A Journal of Educational Studies*, Vol. 6, No. 2 (1975), pp. 41–48; Stanley W. Rothstein, "Orientations: First Impressions in an Urban Junior High School," *Urban Education*, Vol. 14, No. 1 (April 1979), pp. 91–92.

6

The Supervisory Process
and Organizational Change

QUESTIONS TO THINK ABOUT

1. What is the supervisory process?

2. What initial problems make it difficult for supervisors to relate well to their teaching staffs?

3. What are the new structures of supportive supervision?

4. What happens in the weekly individual and group conferences?

5. What is the Focus Interview and how can it help supervisors and staff to learn more about what is happening in their classrooms?

6. Why is it important for teachers to have time to reflect upon the work they are doing with students?

The supervisory process provides staff members with ego support and a way of solving classroom problems. It helps them to grow and develop as professionals and persons. In the process the supervisor uses her skills and knowledge of human behavior and the group process to enable teachers to increase their effectiveness and sensitivity in the classroom. To this task she brings her knowledge of learning environments and theory, her understanding of human development, and her experience.[1] How is she able to share these insights with staff members? The key lies in her understanding and acceptance of herself and those she works with during the school day. The transition from teacher to school leader is a difficult one, requiring an examination of one's self in relation to the new tasks and responsibilities of the administrative position.[2]

INITIAL PROBLEMS

The ability of the supervisor to care about and respond to the behavior and feelings of staff members is the most important skill she can possess. How does she put into effect this supportive way of supervising teachers and other staff? When teachers do not want to participate in the supportive supervision process, what must she do then?

One way to establish supportive supervision is to appeal to staff for their support based on their individual desires to be more successful in their classrooms and the collective opinions and feelings of everyone working inside the school building.[3] The more teachers support the idea of conferencing and problem solving, the more likely they will be to exert peer group control in group conferences. An appeal should also be made to parent and community groups so they can better understand and participate in the changes that take place in their school, and so they can assist in deciding what changes are necessary. This, in turn, provides the professional staff with information about the opinions and attitudes of their "clients."

How does the administrator assume the role of the inquiring facilitator?[4] She has a difficult task, for she must give up her traditional role and behavior in order to assume that of the interested co-professional and colleague. She must begin to build different types of relationships with staff members who are sometimes suspicious and distrustful of school administrators. Her awareness of these attitudes helps her to be patient and to understand that it may take months before she loses the image of the stranger, the manager, and the manipulator. Teachers want to know whether the conferences will be confidential and whether information disclosed there will later be used against them. The school administrator must assure staff of the complete confidentiality of the supervisory conferences. For the skillful supervisor, the most difficult thing will be not to talk too much in these meetings, not to give advice, and not to provide staff members with "insights." It is often difficult for leaders to accept the idea that learning is a process and that teachers should be allowed to make their own decisions and mistakes.[5]

One way of dealing with the anxieties of teachers is to be aware of, and responsive to, their concerns during their intitial meetings. The more sensitive a supervisor is toward these first responses to the conference the better. She should also be acutely aware of her own behavior, the better to diminish the teacher's fears and resistance to change. The idea of open communications in schools may be a revolutionary one for male supervisors and teachers.

Many new administrators have doubts about their ability to supervise. They want to look like cool and competent persons who know what to do in every situation. They often do not want to ask for assistance from others who perhaps know more or could help them to function better.

Moreover, new administrators may be unable to separate themselves from their former identities as teachers. They may find it difficult to tell whether they are helping the teacher too much or too little. They may not be able to determine whether teachers see them as helpful persons or as administrators who must be placated whenever possible.

But there are also bright spots for new administrators. They may have feelings of satisfaction during the very moments that they experience these doubts and anxieties about their performance as supervisors. They may discover some pleasure when they see teachers growing and developing in their professional knowledge and skills; when they see them internalize and use insights gained in supervisory conferences to teach and counsel children more effectively. They may also feel a heightened sense of competency and self-worth. When teachers discover new and better ways to do their work, ways that are better than the ones the supervisor might have suggested, then administrators can feel that they have helped staff to achieve a higher level of professional effectiveness.

Unfortunately, the structure of school supervision today is overly inspection-oriented and bureaucratic. Contacts between administrators and staff are too formal and ritualistic, and conferences occur too infrequently.[6] This makes it difficult for supervisors to go over the work teachers perform each day in their classrooms. Yet supervisors are responsible for everything that occurs in the classrooms, even when they are not on the premises. When things go well, they share the credit, but when things do not go well they often receive a good share of the criticism.

One of the effects of this weak supervisory system is the resentment it generates. Another unfortunate effect is the closed information and communication patterns it encourages. Supervisors are forced to make decisions based on information that is often misleading, inaccurate, or incomplete.

Thinking about human emotions as a blend of positive and negative feelings is an important insight for administrators who want to change bureaucratic organizational structures. Every new supervisor has both negative and positive feelings about the position and responsibilities she shoulders within the school. She can perform the work in the most conscious, dedicated way if she recognizes and accepts these feelings as normal. Denying ambivalent responses to her new position and her relations with teachers is not an effective way to handle such feelings. Denial often causes administrators to act inconsistently. Inconsistent behavior is almost always a sign that the administrator is unaware of, and unconscious of, her real motivations. Only by gaining a deeper insight into their own reasons for acting as they do can school administrators learn to help staff members develop their communication and interpersonal skills and relationships; only then can they gain the friendship and trust of staff members and students.[7]

ADMINISTRATORS AND STAFF

Some supervisors may not know how to help staff improve their communication skills.[8] To change this, supervisors need to understand that the relationship they have with staff members is the most important factor they need to attend to if new and more effective ways of communicating are to be developed in the school organization.

The importance of helping teachers and counselors to make conscious use of themselves in encounters and relationships with students, and with one another, is yet another important function of supervision. Skillful supervisors help staff understand their feelings and preconceptions about what is happening in the classroom and school. For example, teachers learn to change their ways of doing things once they are able to see that their students, though passive and dependent on the surface, have deep feelings about them and their authoritarian behavior.

Nevertheless, a widespread misreading of the supervisory process continues to exist in many schools today. The skillful supervisor needs to accept each staff person in her first meetings with them; she needs to seek information that helps her to understand and respect them. But she does not have to agree with or condone their behaviors when these are not socially or pedagogically acceptable. She needs to learn to separate acceptance of the person from an uncritical acceptance of that person's behaviors.

Most important for effective school leadership is the opportunity that principals and their assistants provide for staff to express and rationalize their feelings about their students, their school, and their supervisors. This involves more than merely allowing teachers to "blow off steam": administrators need to help staff members analyze their emotions. Supervisors must also evaluate their own efforts based on insights they gain from their work with teachers.

However, it is not enough to have teachers talk about their feelings and relations with others. They need to be able to analyze and work through such feelings and the problems they cause. Under no circumstances should these tasks be shifted to the supervisor. Supervisory conferences should help teachers see and understand their own emotions, ambivalence, biases, and needs. Such insights can help them to better understand their relationships with students and others with whom they work. Above all, teachers need to be more aware of the feelings and needs of the children they serve.

When can such discussions take place between supervisors and staff members? Such talks are only possible when the relationship between supervisors and staff members is governed by a sense of mutual acceptance and respect. Inevitably, there will be misunderstandings and mistakes even in the most supportive school environments. Below is an example of a conference in which an administrator helped to make a teacher more conscious of her negative feelings toward one of her students:

"How do you feel about Ellis Dones?"
　"Ellis? Oh, I like him well enough."
　"Yes?"
　(No response.)
　"What do you like most about him?"

"I don't know. I just like him."

"I don't know is not an answer. Think about it. What is it you like about Ellis?"

"I don't know."

"Well then, tell me about his behavior in class. Is he well-behaved?"

"Well, as a matter of fact, he's not in class much."

"He's absent a lot of the time?"

"Yes."

"How is he when he does come to class?"

"Well, he's a bully, you know. Always beating up on some of the smaller kids."

"He bullies the other children?"

"Yes."

"Tell me more."

"Well, he comes late to class when he does come and always makes a grand entrance. He always disrupts the class."

"Does he have any friends in class?"

"No, not really. Most of the kids are afraid of him."

"So he's really a loner in your class?"

"Yeah. I never thought about it but I guess he is."

The conference continued. The teacher mentioned one example after another in which Ellis behaved angrily and defiantly.

"We've been talking about Ellis for more than 20 minutes now, and you haven't said a good word about him. Do you still think you like him?"

The teacher paused and seemed surprised by my remark. Then she said slowly: "I guess I don't really care for him at all."[9]

The remainder of this conference dealt with the teacher's real feelings about Ellis and the ways she responded to him in her classroom. Apparently, without knowing it, she had been accepting her students' view of Ellis and pushing him further into his out-group behavior and his status as a bully to be avoided. Once she understood her feelings of anger and resentment toward Ellis, she was ready to cope with them. She was ready to move toward the boy in an empathetic manner—to get to know him better so she could like him more, so she could see the world through his eyes. He was no longer just a disruptive student and bully. Now he was someone who had no friends in school, someone who awoke each morning and came to a school and classroom where everyone feared and disliked him.

This conference was a helping situation because both the teacher and the supervisor saw it that way. Both knew each other and believed their conferences were making them more conscious and effective in their schoolwork. Both possessed skills in feeling expression and inquiry. The administrator did not evaluate the remarks of the teacher. He only sought clarification, while dismissing defensive responses such as, "I don't know." It was "okay" for the teacher to dislike Ellis Dones, but it was not okay was for her to be unaware of her own feelings. The administrator in this conference did not try to change the teacher's feelings. He only attempted to clarify them by feeding back her statements and perceptions. The supervisor was content to see the classroom world through the eyes of this teacher. His task became one of making her more conscious about aspects of her problem that had escaped her attention in the past. Later, the teacher expressed excitement with the supervisory process and her new insights. She was anxious to try out new approaches to Ellis, even though she understood that there might not be any dramatic changes in his behavior at first. She felt good about the conference because she now felt she had a way of improving her relationship with Ellis. Throughout this conference between two co-professionals, the teacher was the person responsible for describing and analyzing the problem. This meant that the definition of the situation was in her hands and not in those of the administrator. Since the conference dealt with her feelings and concerns in the classroom, the teacher's involvement and interest was assured. Since the solutions to the problem were hers and hers alone, her commitment to the problem solving process was assured.

THE LEARNING PROCESS

If administrators are to succeed in building more effective communication with teachers, they need to view teachers as learners who are facing unknown tasks and challenges in their classrooms. The learning process is never a simple forward motion into deeper insights, knowledge, and skills. Usually, learners tend to move backward into older, more comfortable ways of doing things before they finally become committed to new ideas and behaviors.[10] School leaders need to avoid behaviors that show impatience with this process: acting angry and exasperated is not helpful. Research indicates that learners are involved in a process of give and take in which they find themselves being pulled forward and backward for some time. When the new learnings threaten old associations and understandings, the learner seeks out the older, more familiar knowledge and insights she lived by in the past. Staff can learn things best when supervisors break the new learnings into manageable parts, when they provide teachers with tasks they can do successfully. Teachers want to learn how to become more effective in their classrooms. Yet at the same time that they desire help and direction, they fear the changes such help may bring about.[11]

When teachers go through this learning process, they often increase their professional skills, but they also find that they must change their attitudes, values, and ways of doing things. At first, they may resist these changes and the methods that bring them about; they may be afraid of what administrators will do with their new information; or they may become fearful about what they will learn about themselves, what they may become. Additional problems may develop as teachers gain new insights into their schoolwork and find themselves unable to use their new knowledge effectively. Staff need the opportunity to practice new ways of doing their work; they need to integrate their new insights and learnings slowly.

What can administrators expect when they try to improve their supervision and communication processes?[12] Sometimes they can expect staff to resist, to struggle against the new methods and goals. The behavior of staff members may contradict their statements; they may argue about not having enough time or energy to interact in the new ways while providing peer members with "lip service" support. Sometimes they may use group meetings to discuss their negative feelings only, testing out the attitudes of other staff who may have their own doubts and anxieties about the new processes. Finally, they may show surprise and astonishment when the new methods bring good results, results they hadn't thought possible.

Common sense tells us that there are no hard and fast rules for dealing with the problems of individuals. All of the variables in each situation change constantly: the time frame, the place (as it is experienced in successive events by different people), the behaviors and attitudes of staff and their students, and the responses of administrators.

An effective approach, then, is for administrators to focus attention on the learning process and development of each teacher until they are well understood. Instead of offering advice, the skillful supervisor should provide staff members with ways of helping themselves to work through their difficulties whenever possible. Each innovation or change that staff use in their work forces them to rearrange their old relationships, attitudes, and ways of looking at the world.

When supervisors and staff accept the changes brought about by new and more intensive forms of communication and problem solving, they find themselves giving up familiar ways of thinking and feeling about the school organization; they find themselves giving up ideas and ways of doing things that gave them comfort and support in the past.

For supportive supervision to succeed, the supervisor needs to be certain that she has worked through her own feelings and reasons for acting as she does. Why does she do the things she does? Does she want to dominate her staff? Or have her experiences and thinking made her so passive and distant that she cannot understand or identify with their needs and concerns?

When supervisors try to use themselves in more conscious ways, it often increases the strain and tension they experience at first. When staff are asked to do things differently, they often respond by resisting new concepts and behavior patterns. Administrators should be prepared for a certain amount of free-floating anger, anxiety, and regressive behavior. Some staff may be frightened by the new methods; others may spend their energies griping about them. Some may find it threatening to examine their feelings and those of the youngsters in their classrooms; or they may simply go through the motions of communicating with others, hoping the new ways will finally fail. Obviously, it helps supervisors if they recognize and accept these normal responses to supervision. They need to help staff understand their capacities as well as their limitations. Moreover, it helps administrators if they understand that learning new ways of communicating in schools is difficult, and that staff may have a tendency to be defensive and resistant. Both the supervisor and the teachers need to be prepared to deal with behaviors and communication patterns that seem to indicate resistance. The supervisor has to be ready to help staff understand the meaning of their own behavior, as part of their professional development toward performing their educational services more responsively.

Research indicates that individuals don't always communicate their feelings through language alone. Often, because they are anxious and afraid, they show their resistance to supervision through inattention or passivity.[13] Submitting written reports or evaluations may be done poorly, or not at all. The teacher may complain about "not having enough time" or "not seeing the value" of the conferences. Often, what they may really be saying is that they do not wish to participate. They may say this by being uncommunicative about their feelings, or they may be late or miss the meeting entirely. They may talk only about their own rationalizations, excuses, and explanations of events without focusing on their own actions and motivations in problem situations.

Staff may disagree with procedures and methods, or they may try to talk only about nonthreatening topics of curriculum and pedagogy rather than the emotional relationships they develop with students. Such attitudes and behaviors should be used by skillful supervisors to set the initial agendas for individual conferences: the development of a supervisory relationship and experiences that help teachers increase their abilities to make conscious use of themselves in their classroom work. This is done by deepening the teachers' insights into their own feelings and motivations and those of their students. The following is an example of how unconscious attitudes and feelings can undercut the best intentions of supervisors and teachers:

Report #1 (October 21)

This morning, Ms. Smith, a former student of mine at Hunter College, came to see me after having tried my methods in a nearby junior high school in the South Bronx. She got right to the point, telling me I was a fraud. All my techniques didn't work at all! She had tried them for months and things were getting worse in her classes. She was very upset and angry. "I try to be understanding. I try to ask questions, but they don't answer me! They don't respond!" Since this woman had been one of my most enthusiastic students, I asked if I could observe her in action at her school.

Report #2 (October 24)

Ms. Smith worked with a teenager from one of her classes this morning. She asked him about an incident she was upset about and kept demanding that he explain how he felt about acting so badly. "Did you really think it was okay to act like that? Did you?" she asked in an angry voice. Instead of reflecting an accepting and friendly relationship with the boy, her voice and posture were full of defiance. The student responded to her questions with one-word answers, and this woman dutifully struggled through the five stages of the Focus Interview method. When it was over, both were tired and upset, and Ms. Smith wrote out a pass, telling the youngster to go back to his class. As soon as he was gone, she turned to me. "See! Nothing! The questioning doesn't seem to work with these kinds of children!" I sat next to her and said: "You're very angry with that boy, aren't you?" And Ms. Smith began to cry. We talked for a long time about her feelings as a new teacher in a difficult school and about the help she was receiving from others. She found it hard to understand or be at ease with minority and immigrant children (she had always lived in the suburbs), and she was overly concerned with being liked by them. She was overcome with doubts and fears and felt little satisfaction with her classroom work. She was able to see that her own anger and frustration were turning her conferences into inquisitions. She agreed to work with me on a weekly basis for a while so we could improve her situation. I told her to stop conferencing youngsters and begin to talk to them casually in the playground, lunchroom, or after school. I urged her to meet some of their parents in their homes and to get to know the leaders and followers in her classes as well as she could. Then we spent the rest of the time talking about her feelings toward her students, especially those who were challenging her authority in the classroom. We made some progress and decided to meet again in a week.

Report #3 (October 28)

We made better progress today. Ms. Smith had an interesting insight: "You know," she said, "We work so well together! I think it's because we like each other so much."[14] Now that Ms. Smith has someone to talk to, she is identifying her problems in more detail, and she is beginning to solve some of them. She still has difficulties in understanding minority and poor children, but she has faced these difficulties and made a decision to overcome them. Her anger and frustration seem to have lessened, and she has befriended several of her students. Word of her visits to the homes of youngsters spread like wildfire. She now has a reputation as a teacher who is different from the others and seems to care about her students.[15]

After a few weeks of these conferences, we both felt Ms. Smith had passed the critical point in her teaching career. She was wrong, though, in her first remarks to me. The conferencing system worked well in an inner-city school when it was tried by trained, experienced persons.

Staff increase their knowledge and skills when they accept the idea of learning as a process that must begin where they are in their own intellectual and emotional development. When teachers understand that supervisors accept them as they are and expect them to move forward from that point, supportive supervision becomes possible. When they accept the idea that supervisors will not measure their schoolwork against that of others, or against standards that were preferred in the past, a trusting relationship can begin. This process of supervision and evaluation permits teachers to abandon their previous defensive orientations and begin to think reflectively about their classwork.

Time is used purposefully and precisely in the school setting, because it is impossible to schedule hundreds of thousands of people without developing timetables. The school administrator needs to help staff members accept the responsibility of coming to conferences on time and submitting records and reports when they are due. She has to discuss and analyze the psychological implications when they fail to work within these parameters.

The skillful supervisor communicates concern and acceptance of the schoolwork of staff through her attitude and behavior. She helps teachers see that mistakes are natural and inevitable in a good learning environment: they do not indicate failure. Rather, they are important moments in the learning process during which teachers, students, and supervisors can deepen their knowledge and skills through the analysis and planning of more effective ways of doing their schoolwork.

THE STRUCTURE OF SUPERVISION: SCHEDULED CONFERENCES

Enlightened supervision has a structure that is quite different from what one sees in the schools today. The "how-to" of supportive supervision is learned in the weekly individual and group conferences between supervisors and staff members. Considering the irrational organizational structure of traditional schools, it is not surprising that so many school administrators throw up their hands and say, "There is no way I can schedule 60 or more conferences with staff each week." This may be true. However, such conferences must be held, even if they require creative scheduling. Supervisors can begin by meeting only with teachers who are interested in new ways of working together.

Once the supervisor decides to begin holding conferences with staff members, she needs to clarify their purposes. Often the purpose can be stated quite simply: teachers come to their positions with university degrees, knowledge, and skills; but the school system expects them to update and deepen these insights and understandings. It expects them to develop new skills. Therefore it provides staff development activities and supervisors whose primary task is to help teachers perform their classwork more effectively.

A supervisor has to make choices if she works in a traditional setting. Whom should she select for such training? Who among the staff would like to volunteer?

Since conferences need to be held regularly and require preparation by both supervisors and staff members, it may not be feasible to hold conferences with all teachers. Later, as more teachers show an interest in participating, new methods will have to be developed to free them so they can have time to reflect on the ways in which they deliver their professional services to children.[16]

THE INDIVIDUAL CONFERENCE

Individual conferences need to be carefully planned by both the supervisor and the teacher. As the school's legally appointed authority, the school administrator needs to focus the discussions on how the teacher is interacting with children in her classroom. Does she know them well? What does she know about them? Who are the youngsters she knows little or nothing about? Why has she neglected these students? Who are the leaders in her classrooms? The followers? Are there any outcasts? What does she do to integrate these outsiders into the mainstream of the class? Does she merely legitimate their unhappy condition by casting them further out because of their poor work or behavior?

How sensitive is she to the feelings of her students? How encouraging? How nonpunitive? Often it is necessary for school administrators to talk about the behavior of students in problem situations. What was the meaning of their behavior? What were they trying to say when they did what they did? Who acted badly? What did the teacher do? Why did she do it? These questions provide markers for staff members in their work with children, guidelines that can help teachers understand what is expected of them in a new situation. The task of supervisors is to focus the discussion of the conference on the role and behavior of the staff member and her students. She should not allow the conference to be diluted by talk about nonrelated matters or generalizations that do not deal with the staff member's actions inside her classroom. While in this conference between co-professionals, the supervisor has specific tasks she must accomplish. She is the inquiring facilitator, and the teacher is the one who needs to identify and discuss important classroom matters. At first, the administrator may take responsibility for deciding on the agenda for these conferences. However, she never focuses the discussion on matters that are of interest only to her. The feedback a supervisor receives from these conferences becomes more valuable as the staff member enters into the supervisory process more fully and gains insights and skills into her own motivations and those of the children she serves.

These individual conferences are the heart and soul of supportive supervision. They are the places where staff members sit down with supervisors to reflect upon and improve the ways they do their classwork. Skillful supervisors help teachers to better understand their own motivations and the behavior and needs of their students. Who are "in" people and what groups do they belong to in the classroom? What are the needs of individuals in these groups? What are their interests and concerns? What problems, if any, do they represent for the school community or staff member? What tensions do they create?

Through the use of questions, the skillful supervisor helps staff to understand how they are helping or hindering students. How can teachers be more effective, more conscious in the way they use themselves with students? What are the reasons for their lack of success in dealing with particular problems? Proactive planning can also play a part in these meetings, helping teachers to analyze the individual and group needs of their students. In all of these discussions, the focus is on the staff member's behavior and role in the classroom situation. What did she do when the problem first surfaced? How did she do it? How did she react to the students? Why did she act in that way? What were her feelings toward the students who were involved in the incident? How did the students feel? How does she evaluate her own behavior and actions? Based on knowledge and skills she has recently acquired about herself, how might she react more effectively?

This is the focus the skillful supervisor needs to maintain; she needs to help staff delve more deeply into all parts of their interactions with others in the school. When necessary, she helps staff members think through things they did not consider before. Still, it is the teacher who reflects upon these events; it is

the staff member who makes judgments about them and suggests ways of improving things.

At the end of the individual conference, the staff member draws up a written
plan of action about what she intends to do in order to solve her problems. She
becomes the responsible person in the problem situation, the one who must put
into action her own plan to improve her classroom situation.[17]

Rather than engage in classoom visitations, the supervisor should rely upon
these conferences and on the written reports teachers bring to them for discussion and analyses. Visitations disturb the relationships between teachers and
students, and between individuals and groups in the classroom. Research shows
that no supervisor enters a classroom without seriously affecting the way that
teachers and students interact.[18] However, the organizational and teaching practices of the nineteenth century die hard. It is therefore difficult for supervisors
to see teachers as they really are in their classrooms; it is difficult to observe
the educational and emotional relationships between teachers and students. The
supervisory visitation itself confounds the process: the staff member does not
act normally. The students also act very differently than they would if the school
supervisor was not in the room evaluating their behavior and that of their
teacher. When school administrators make the legally mandated visitation, they
unwittingly undercut the teacher and relieve her of her responsibility for the
classroom situation. This intervention makes the teacher less likely to be aware
of, or to discuss, serious learning and relational problems with supervisors since
the observation usually changes her behavior and that of her students. Everyone
wants to do their best, everyone wants to look good in front of the principal.
In supportive supervision, the supervisor sees the classroom through the eyes
and ears of the teacher. The supervisor has the knowledge and skills to help
teachers recall and analyze the happenings of the recent past with clarity and
accuracy. Classroom observations of teachers place them in the role of the student in front of their students; they cast them in the role of the learner who
needs to be inspected and corrected by her superiors.

Informational meetings to solve specific problems can use the Focus Interview
as a way of placing teachers and counselors at the center of their own problem
identification-resolution cycle.[19] How is this interview different from other problem solving systems? How can it help teachers to be more effective in their
classwork? The difference is in the conferencing that goes on regularly each
week. This allows staff and supervisors to identify and resolve classroom problems in a more conscious and reflective way. New communication patterns make
it easier for staff to fit together the pieces of their own personal identities and
the needs and expectations of the school organization.

The supervisory conferences must be planned with the functions of the human
ego (the part of the human personality that serves the adaptive processes)[20] kept
firmly in mind; they need to be used as a helping tool rather than an evaluation
instrument. These conferences help staff test new situations and preconceptions
against their own suppositions, to remember things, to focus attention on par-

ticular problems, and to direct conscious and unconscious behaviors. Yet the ego is only a part of the structure that governs human personality and tends to operate on both the conscious and unconscious levels. Can supervisors bring the feelings of teachers to the surface where their inner control structures can exert control over them? Those who have studied these processes say yes.[21]

Much of the structure of supportive supervision is devoted to maintaining a teacher's equilibrum in the school. By using the conferencing method, teachers are often able to identify their needs and concerns more accurately and develop inner controls over their emotions and behavior. By verbalizing their feelings and internalizing them, they begin a process of neutralization that strengthens their control structures (egos) and makes them better able to understand their associations and surroundings.

THE FOCUS INTERVIEW

The importance of the relationship between the supervisor and her staff member needs to be reemphasized. At every moment of the school day, the supervisor needs to be involved in a trusting, friendly association with her teachers. This bond between them needs to be strengthened by constant open two-way communications.

How does the skillful supervisor help staff plan and execute their schoolwork? Teachers need to be urged to monitor themselves, to listen actively to others, and to act in accordance with the insights they develop in the weekly supervisory conferences.

Five objectives are generally served by using the Focus Interview.[22] First, it generates a great deal of information for the supervisor: raw data, which often provides the school administrator with feelings and perspectives she might otherwise not notice. Second, it allows supervisors and teachers to focus on their feelings and behavior as these are affecting classroom practices. This helps teachers become more sensitive to their own feelings and to those of the students they serve. Third, focus interviews help staff see the world through the eyes of the supervisor and the children they serve. Since these children are sometimes problem children the teacher dislikes or distrusts, questions about the students' feelings encourage teachers to use themselves more consciously, to move toward these youngsters to learn more about them. However, students will not reveal themselves to teachers for whom they do not have feelings of trust and friendship. The Focus Interview helps teachers develop trusting relationships. A fourth objective of the interview is to encourage teachers to identify their problems in greater detail so they can be resolved. A final objective is to help supervisors understand and analyze the problem of trust in schools. Trust means more than mere predictability of behavior. It implies friendliness and mutual acceptance, while distrust carries with it attitudes of unfriendliness. When is the behavior of teachers and students a mask and when is it a representation of inner feelings and inclinations?[23] This question cannot be answered until supervisors and staff develop open communications and good personal relationships with each other.

CONTENT AND PROCESS

The Focus Interview consists of a cluster of questions that seek to identify the problems and emotional relationships in classrooms. At the conclusion of each interview session, the supervisor asks the teacher to commit herself to specific lines of action the supervisor has suggested. The supervisor asks probing questions to uncover all the features of the problem. By this method, the administrator can get a better idea about what is happening inside the school building. She can also get a better idea about the way staff respond to students in particular situations.

Cluster 1 Questions: What was the problem? Who was involved? What did the staff member do? How did she do it? What did students do? How did the staff member react to their behavior?

These questions are asked after the teacher has been put at ease. A funneling technique is used to direct the conversation, more and more, away from generalities toward more specific kinds of interaction problems.

Cluster 2 Questions: Does the teacher like the students involved in the problem situation? If so, what does she like about them? What doesn't she like? How do students feel about the teacher? About other students in the class?

This last question cannot be answered with assurance because there is no way that a teacher can know for certain how students feel about her unless they have openly and honestly voiced their feelings. To understand how students feel, the teacher needs to move toward these youngsters so she can learn more about them. The likelihood that students will respond honestly to the teacher's queries will depend upon the relationship that exists between them. If students think the teacher will be angry or vindictive, they will probably not be truthful. Therefore, teachers have to know their students better. They need to become more knowledgeable and more accepting of their students so they can learn who they are and how they are reacting to classroom life. The projective question at the end of this cluster alerts teachers to the fact that everyone has complete consciousness, and that even when student respond to teachers passively, they may have other feelings that adversely affect the learning process.

The verbalization of feelings encourages staff (and students) to be themselves in school and to learn to value open forms of communication. It is also important in helping teachers cope with negative and ambivalent feelings that often go unspoken and unresolved in classroom interactions.

Cluster 3 Questions: Did the teacher feel the others acted in correct ways? Did they themselves do the "right" thing? How did students respond to the teacher's intervention?

These questions ask teachers to think about and to commit themselves to actions they think may improve the problem-situation.

Cluster 4 Questions: How are the staff persons going to improve things? What are they going to do, specifically? How will they do it? What will they do if the problem reappears?

These questions imply that some of the solutions will work and some will not. Unsuccessful solutions will become the focus of further analysis and discussion at the next weekly conference.

The supportive supervision system has five major components: (1) the acceptance of the staff member's feelings, level of attainment, and thoughts; (2) the idea that the teacher has the right and the duty to decide how she will solve her problems; (3) the belief that the staff member should be allowed to choose the way she does her work, subject only to a self-evaluation and the evaluation of her peers and supervisor; (4) the delivery of mutual, ongoing feedback to all teachers so they can know how they are doing during the school year; and (5) the development of self-concepts that encourage teachers (and students) to act with initiative and self-confidence.

Some of the advantages supervisors can expect from this method are:

1. *Information Feedback*: There is an opportunity to develop an atmosphere that is conducive to the exchange of information, feelings, and opinions. The supervisor has an opportunity to relate to the behaviors of the staff as well as to educational content material.

2. *Shared Task Involvement*: There is an opportunity to discuss issues and problems emanating from higher authority or everyday situations. Individuals have a better chance to become more conscious of their own actions, feelings, and attitudes as they discuss them in weekly conferences.

3. *Situational Analysis*: It is possible during the interview to analyze situations in terms of the emotional relationships that are forming in classrooms.

4. *Maintaining Organizational Structure*: It is possible to supervise teachers on a regular basis so they get a sense of the process of problem solving over time. The supervisor works through the staff member without taking over the work function, without showing her how.

5. *Contact*: It is possible to provide regular meeting times for a discussion of common problems, for a period of reflection on what is being done, and how it is succeeding in classrooms.

6. *Directing the Work of Others*: There is an opportunity for the administrator to help staff focus their goals and the methods needed to achieve them.

7. *Responsiveness*: There is an opportunity for supervisors to listen sensitively to staff with a view toward helping them. As teachers and counselors become more aware of their feelings and the feelings of those they serve, they learn to use themselves in more conscious ways.

8. *Interviewing*: There is an opportunity for supervisors to refrain from directive leadership. Directions and advice are not necessary. On the other hand, questions permit staff to express concerns and clarify problems.

The drawbacks of using a conferencing method relate to the organizational structures of present-day public schools, with teacher and supervisor work loads and physical space for interviews. Some of the problems the supervisor encounters in the conferences may be beyond her ability or training. Moreover, it is difficult to generalize from the data of interviews, especially when one supervisor is responsible for many teachers.[24]

GROUP SUPERVISORY CONFERENCES

Group conferences are important because they complement individual staff meetings.[25] These groups, which can be convened at the discretion of the school supervisor, usually consist of five or six teachers who have common interests and responsibilities in the school. Cooperative planning is best worked on in these meetings. When the supervisor is not working with large numbers of individuals, she can hold regularly scheduled weekly group meetings. A period of resistant, defensive behavior sometimes characterizes the first attempts to get these conferences off the ground. Many teachers are too anxious or defensive to engage in new ways of cooperating with fellow staff members. They want to develop a relationship with their administrator that shows them and their work in the best light. Since these attitudes are sometimes strongest among newcomers, they should not be asked to participate in these ventures until they have developed secure relations with their supervisors and fellow staff members.

The skillful supervisor determines when staff are ready to participate in group conferences. Staff need to see the value of sharing the supervision they receive; they need to become aware of why sharing is important. Often, the supervisor may call such meetings so that staff members can discuss common problems and new knowledge and skills.

Report #4

My confidence in the group supervisory approach grew as I watched it in action today. At the weekly staff conference, the lead teacher said she had a confession to make. All of us moved uneasily in our seats. Then she told us she did not know how to teach individualized reading. This was a bombshell because the reading center was a replication of other projects, and individualized reading was the cornerstone of these state programs. One by one, the other teachers stood and admitted that they also used the old ability grouping method for instruction. They also had little or no idea how an individualized reading program was supposed to be taught. This was an important moment in the history of this reading project. Certificated teachers were telling one another they didn't know how to teach according to the mandates of their state-funded replication project. I listened to each person carefully. Then when everyone had spoken, the director asked what they were going to do about it. The groundwork had been laid for an intensive study of the methods and philosophy of individualized instruction in reading. First the lead teacher, and then the others, committed themselves to an in-service training program to learn these new skills. The impetus had come from the teachers themselves. They were the ones who felt the need, and they were the ones who were going to develop the needed skills.[26]

The supervisor may determine that a discussion about what needs to be done in situations that are common to all members of the group is necessary. She may want to see how staff members work with one another. She may feel that she will better understand them if she observes them in this kind of group supervisory situation.

Group supervisory conferences should have an organization and a declared purpose that is strengthened by the weekly meetings. At first, these purposes may be determined by supervisors, as in initial individual conferences. As staff become more accustomed to the purposes and methods used, they should be asked to make contributions to the agenda; later, they may take control of the entire process and use supervisors as resource persons.

A supervisor in these kinds of conferences needs to know how certain staff use these meetings for their own ends. Some teachers use the group as an avenue for avoiding any talk about themselves and their actions inside the school building. They are resistant to, and afraid of, skill development that seeks to raise their consciousness levels. They are apprehensive about the closeness that can develop between them and their supervisors. Still, the group conference is an excellent tool for providing staff members with insights and skills about the group process. It gives teachers the chance to work together on some of their common concerns and anxieties.

How does the skillful supervisor begin these discussions? Usually she informs the group about the content that will be dealt with during each session. Then she asks a question that begins the conversation. As staff discuss the content of the group conference, the supervisor tries to keep silent, unless the group needs more information or the discussion seems to fizzle. In such meetings the supervisor observes who talks and who is quiet, and she sometimes steps into the discussion to ask the quiet ones for their thoughts or feelings. Also, supervisors may take it upon themselves to summarize points and decisions as they are made in the conference. This can help staff members see what was decided and where things seem to be headed. There is usually a final summation by the supervisor, during which new problems and issues are brought to the attention of the group as matters for study during future meetings.

One outcome of this method is that staff are made more aware of one another's problems; a second is that teachers gain new insight into their own problems and the problems of co-workers. Such meetings need to do more than merely allow teachers to see that they are not alone in having classroom difficulties. The supervisor needs to help staff members devise strategies for solving their problems; she needs to make certain teachers leave these meetings with concrete suggestions for action.

There are staff who, because of the support they receive from others, express angry and hostile attitudes they did not reveal in earlier supervisory conferences.

The skillful supervisor needs to encourage these angry ones to express their disagreements, especially if the group seems able to accept them.

Other staff members may say very little in group discussions, hiding their feelings by only listening or responding in monosyllables or short answers. The individual conference needs to be used to help these teachers to speak up more. Because the group is made up of individuals who sometimes have closer relations with the administrator than with one another, the supervisor needs to encourage all participants to share their insights and feelings and to use the group as a support system that helps teachers grow and develop personally and professionally.

A final example of an actual case history may help explain what happens when the supervisory process works well.

Report #5

Today I met Mr. Stern, our new replacement for class 8-4. He is fresh out of college where he was originally a pre-law student. His counselor at the university suggested he take some education courses as a hedge. Now he has been assigned to me on the fourth floor, and he seems to understand that he is in a tough situation.

Monday I met with Mr. Stern for our first supervisory conference. I told Mr. Stern we would meet once a week and that Thursday afternoons he could join a group of new teachers that met after school. These statements were greeted with relief. Mr. Stern was happy for the support, but he was anxious too. He wanted to know what we would be doing in these supervisory sessions. But he did agree to work with me despite his anxieties; he did accept my offer of help. I told him we would try to identify and resolve his day-to-day classroom problems.

Here are some of the notes I took about this new teacher: What do I want to accomplish with him? I want to help him see himself and his minority and poor students in terms of the processes they are going through so he can provide them with greater acceptance and support. Even with the most angry youngsters threatening the authority of this new teacher, a supportive attitude seemed best. I wanted him to send a message to his students: I see what you are doing. I'm going to work with you until we both learn to accept each other; until we both learn to behave in new and more satisfying ways.

I met with Mr. Stern today. We worked on his feelings about teaching a subject he knows very little about to children who weren't interested anyway. How did he feel about what was happening in his classroom? How did he feel about each child? What did he know about them? What did he like about them? What didn't he like? These questions made Mr. Stern aware of something he had not thought about: he was going to be asked about what was happening to him, he was going to be asked how well he knew his students and how well he liked them. Did he know which students were friends with one another after school? (He did not, but he decided to find out.) Did he know which children were outsiders without anyone to talk to? (He was able to name a few.) Which of his students were the leaders? Which the followers? Mr. Stern began to talk quite knowledgeably about groups that he had discovered by himself. I asked him why there were some children he did not know at all? (He promised to get to know them all.) By asking these questions, I hoped to focus his attention on his own actions in the classroom. What was he doing in there? Why was he doing those things? How was he doing it? How did his behavior make him feel? (He felt ineffective and angry with those youngsters who were disrupting his lessons.) How did students feel about him as a teacher? Of course, Mr. Stern could only guess at the answer to this question. There was no way for him to know unless they told him, and there wasn't that much communication between them.

By the next Monday meeting, Mr. Stern began to make up some of the agenda for our meeting. I usually added one or two items. An early meeting dealt with the problems of classroom discipline, a perennial topic in this inner-city junior high school. Mr. Stern recalled that, in his group session, he was able to give and receive feedback on his feelings about students and about me. He was able to share his feelings and insights. But he felt that his failures in the school were related mostly to his poor training at the university; no one prepared him for the anger, despair, and apathy of his students or fellow teachers. His first efforts were dominated by his memories of junior high school as it had existed when he was a student. In approaching his teaching in this way, he was ignoring the unique biographies of his students; his own impressionistic interpretations of them, and the kind of persons they were supposed to be, were not very flattering. We probed deeply into his preconceptions to see how he sometimes determined his own actions in classroom situations. He felt blameworthy and ashamed that he could not maintain order and control in his classes. He felt humiliated too. We were unable to deal effectively with these feelings at first.

Wednesday, our supervisory conference focused on the lessons Mr. Stern was teaching his eighth graders. "How did your lesson go?" I asked.

"Fine."

I asked him to tell me more about it. Then I asked him when the lessons seemed to go wrong. He was able to pinpoint moments when he became confused, and when the students seemed to lose interest. Asking him about this helped him realize how he could have improved things, and he wrote some of his ideas down on paper. By now, Mr. Stern realizes that the only realities we deal with are the ones that he brings to the conference. Still, he asked me when I would be coming into his classroom to observe a lesson. He was surprised when I told him that might not be the best way to improve his teaching ability. I wanted to see things through his eyes only; I wanted him to be our eyes and ears in the classroom situation, our primary source of information. I knew that because of our growing relationship, by using questioning methods, I could get him to be more conscious about what was happening in his classroom.

At a later meeting, I wrote in my notes that Mr. Stern was beginning to take his role as the responsible person seriously. He was remembering much of what was happening in the classroom. Today he spoke more openly about his feelings and attitudes toward some of his fellow staff. He was angry with administrators who came into his room and momentarily restored order. He was upset because, when they left the room, the disorder began again and he was unable to contain it. He was also unhappy with his lessons, which were mostly from textbooks or workbooks and seldom interesting to his students. I told him to focus on those things that were bothering him most; then I asked about ways we could make things better. Although he studied at the City University, Mr. Stern felt he was woefully unprepared to teach in the junior high school. He was angry at the school administration too, because he had been assigned to teach a subject (Social Studies) he was not licensed to teach and which he knew little about. He was unable to do anything more than lecture, while his students copied notes or silently read from the text.

I encouraged him to share these problems with teachers in his group supervisory conference and to think about ways of improving his teaching.

Notes from a subsequent meeting: We are ready to begin a new stage in Mr. Stern's training. Today we were able to discuss his feelings in depth because we have grown to like each other. He has finally accepted the idea that there is no one way to do his work. The problems we work on now are almost always chosen by Mr. Stern. In addition, he decides how to improve his classroom situation. He feels that slowly things are getting better because of our meetings. He asked me to talk more about myself and my problems as a new assistant principal. He wants to know more about me. I told him how I came here instead of to the model school I was supposed to be assigned to.

Mr. Stern asked me to visit his class the second period so I could see the improvement. I did and was surprised at how much better things seem to be. Monitors took attendance while the class worked at their desks and waited for Mr. Stern to begin his lesson. Then Mr. Stern discussed the differences between the Civil Rights Revolution, the Women's Rights Revolution, and the American Revolution. There was a great deal of interest and discussion, and the students decided that a revolution was not a revolution if there wasn't any bloodshed.

Mr. Stern has decided to visit some of his students in their homes, in spite of the apparent danger. After all, this is the South Bronx, and there are 70 fires here every evening. He is also using class experiences and field trips to develop an experience-based curriculum. His teaching is getting better, and he seems to feel better about things. He's still focusing on the moments when things don't go well, but there seem to be fewer of those moments.

Our group conference today discussed the teacher's role in providing youngsters with more support and acceptance in the classroom. Mr. Stern brought up the idea of codifying some of the group's ideas for other staff. This is what they came up with. All students have consciousness and feelings and should be freed from traumatic handling in the school. All are unique individuals who must be treated differentially and with respect. The relationship between staff and students is the most important element in the learning situation. All student and teacher behavior is meaningful and deserving of reflection and thought.

Summary report of the fall term: Mr. Stern has developed some important interpersonal skills. He is able to express his feelings about others in descriptive, non-threatening ways. He is able to talk about feelings and about problems he has with fellow staff members and students. He is more conscious of his hostile feelings toward authority figures. He told me he has just realized that some of the supervisors are as lost as he was when he began his teaching experience. "They could use a few good conferences, couldn't they?" he said with a smile. Because of his new inquiry skills, he is better able to help his students understand their own behavior. In the beginning, Mr. Stern had great difficulty talking about his attitudes and feelings. Now he is better able to empathize with students; he is better able to clarify some of his own psychological scripts that get in the way of good communication. He is encouraging his students to explore and understand their experiences and to search for deeper meanings in them. Even the problem of racism, which is a constant, is being used by him to create greater awareness and self-respect in his minority students.[27]

SUMMARY

Initial problems of supervisors are usually related to their own sense of competency and their need to develop good relations with staff members. The relations between teachers and administrators are sometimes strained, and staff development efforts are often shallow. New structures of supportive supervision are important if teachers are to have the time and ability to reflect upon their work with students. The "how-to" of this support system is developed in weekly individual and group conferences where teachers learn to become more conscious of what they are doing, how they are doing it, and what effect their actions are having on students. Feelings also have a strong effect upon the teacher-learner relationship. It is only when teachers face themselves and their feelings that they become truly conscious inside the classroom. Supportive supervision is an ongoing process in which teachers learn to identify and resolve the problems they confront each day.

ACTIVITIES

1. Choose someone you like and trust to become your supervisor for a few weeks. Discuss the problems you are having in your school and classroom and write out three or four things you can do to make things better. Then do those things and meet with this person again. How successful was this method? Were there things you tried that didn't work?

2. Study the parts of the Focus Interview mentioned in this chapter. Then choose a student you are not doing well with and make him your special project. Move toward him and try to get to know more about him. Spend some time talking to him one-on-one and make it a point to always recognize and greet him each day. Use the cluster of questions from the Focus Interview to find out how this student is getting along inside the school. What does he like? What bothers him? Does he have any friends in your class? If so, who are they? What do they like to do? If not, why not? Then write a report telling the class what happened when you changed your behavior toward this youngster.

NOTES

1. W. Kimball, "Supervision," in C. W. Harris (ed.), *Encyclopedia of Educational Research*, 3rd ed. (New York: MacMillan, 1960), p. 1442; G. Egan, *The Skilled Helper: A Systematic Approach to Effective Helping* (Pacific Grove, Calif.: Brooks/Cole Publishing Company, 1990), pp. 48–49

2. G. A. Kimble, "Psychology's Two Cultures," *American Psychologist*, Vol. 39 (1984), pp. 833–839; D. Johnson and F. Johnson, *Joining Together* (Englewood Cliffs, N.J.: Prentice-Hall, 1982), pp. 203–233; Stanley W. Rothstein, "The First Supportive Environment," *The Clearing House*, Vol. 50, No. 8 (April 1977), pp. 357–360.

3. Rothstein, "The First Supportive Environment," pp. 357–360. Robert G. Owens, *Organizational Behavior in Education* (Boston: Allyn & Bacon, 1995), pp. 176–182.

4. Stanley W. Rothstein, "The Tip of the Iceberg: Teacher Distrust of Administrators," *The Clearing House*, Vol. 53, No. 5 (January 1980), 42–46.

5. Stanley W. Rothstein and A. E. Dubin, "Ego Support in a Supportive Environment," *The Guidance Clinic* (February 1984), pp. 14–16; Stanley W. Rothstein, "Supportive Supervision: Leadership for the 21st Century," in Andrew Dubin (ed.), *Leadership for the 21st Century* (London: Falmar Press, 1991), pp. 150–164.

6. Julia T. Wood, *Relational Communication* (Belmont, Calif.: Wadsworth Publishing Company, 1995), pp. 225–250; F. Herzberg, *Work and the Nature of Man* (Cleveland, Ohio: World Book, 1966); Chris Argyris, "Interpersonal Barriers to Decision Making," *Harvard Business Review*, No. 44 (1996), pp. 84–97.

7. M. L. Knapp, *Nonverbal Communication in Human Interaction* (New York: Holt, Rinehart and Winston, 1978), pp. 75–79; Rothstein, "Ego Support in a Supportive Environment," pp. 11–16; Stanley W. Rothstein, "Conflict Resolution in a Supportive Environment," *Education and Urban Society* (February 1975).

8. Stanley W. Rothstein, "Building and Maintaining High Trust Climates: Training the New Administrator in Feeling Expression and Inquiry Skills," *Education and Urban Society* (November 1976), pp. 81–101.

9. B. Joyce, R. Hersh, and M. McKibbin, *The Structure of School Improvement* (New York: Longman, 1983), pp. 88–89; William G. Thomas, "Experiential Education—A Rationale for Creative Problem Solving," *Education and Urban Society* (February 1975), pp. 172–181.

10. Argyris, "Interpersonal Barriers to Decision-Making," pp. 84–97.

11. F. H. Kanfer and A. P. Goldstein (eds.), *Helping People Change: A Textbook of Methods* (New York: Pergamon Press, 1986), pp. 112–134; Rothstein, "Conflict Resolution in a Supportive Environment."

12. From my field notes.

13. E. E. Jones, J. D. Cumming, and M. J. Horowitz, "Another Look at the Nonspecific Hypothesis of Therapeutic Effectiveness," *Journal of Consulting and Clinical Psychology*, Vol. 56 (1988), pp. 40–47; M. J. Mahoney and D. B. Arnkoff, "Cognitive and Self-Control Therapies," in S. L. Garfield and A. E. Bergin, (eds.), *Handbook of Psychotherapy and Behavior Change* (New York: Wiley, 1978).

14. E. Jacobson, *The Self and the Object World* (New York: International Universities Press, 1964), pp. 19–33.

15. L. M. Miller, *American Spirit: Visions of a New Corporate Culture* (New York: Morrow, 1984), pp. 211–214.

16. Rothstein, "Conflict Resolution in a Supportive Environment."

17. From my field notes.

18. J. E. Robertshaw and M. N. Rerick, *Problem-Solving: A Systems Approach* (New York: Petrocelli Books, 1978); G. D. Gottfredson, "A Theory-Ridden Approach to Program Evaluation," *American Psychologist*, Vol. 39 (1984), pp. 1101–1112.

19. Stanley W. Rothstein, "The Focus Interview," *The Guidance Clinic* (December 1981), pp. 357–360.

20. R. Driscoll, *Pragmatic Psychotherapy* (New York: Van Nostrand Reinhold, 1984), pp. 22–25.

21. F. H. Kanfer and B. K. Schefft, *Guiding Therapeutic Change* (Champaign, Ill.: Research Press, 1988), pp. 37–39.

22. M. A. Lieberman, "Social Supports: The Consequences of Psychologizing: A Commentary," *Journal of Consulting and Clinical Psychology*, Vol. 54 (1991), pp. 461–465.

23. W. H. Cormier and L. S. Cormier, "Choice or Change: Issues of Clients and How to Work with Them," *Journal of Counseling and Human Service Professions*, Vol. 1, No. 1 (1986), pp. 88–99.

24. J. G. Bruhn and A. S. Gurman, "Measuring Social Support: A Synthesis of Current Approaches," *Journal of Behavioral Medicine*, Vol. 7 (1984), pp. 151–169; A. Ellis, *Overcoming Resistance: Rational-Emotive Therapy with Difficult Clients* (New York: Springer, 1985).

25. E. E. Emery, "Empathy: Psychoanalytic and Client-Centered," *American Psychologist*, Vol. 42 (1987), pp. 513–515; F. J. Dorn (ed.), *The Social Influence Process in Counseling and Psychotherapy* (Springfield, Ill.: Charles C. Thomas, 1986).

26. From my field notes.

27. From my field notes.

7

The Administrative Process

QUESTIONS TO THINK ABOUT

1. What is the administrative process, and why is it important?
2. What is democratic administration, and how does it differ from more traditional forms of management?
3. Why is it important to select staff that have the potential for open communications systems?
4. Why is it important to hire and train paraprofessionals?
5. How can democratic administrative structures be set up in your school?

Although most administrators agree that the climate of a school is deeply affected by what they do, few make this a topic of intensive study.[1] While there are many reasons for this, two deserve our attention: (1) teachers and administrators continue to do their work as they were taught when they were students, and (2) in the minds of some, it is not possible to do more than react to the many unforeseen pressures and events that occur each day in our overcrowded, underfunded schools.

Most school districts have boards of education that set up the administrative and organizational structures under which staff do their work. A recent study found that a district's values and norms establish learning standards and methods in schools.[2] Staff also bring preexisting ideas to these situations. In schools, administration is traditionally the function of a specific, licensed group of people; seldom is it the shared responsibility of certificated staff. Teachers function in cellular classrooms that afford them much autonomy. However, outside the classroom the administrative structures are controlled by boards of education and the supervisory personnel they employ. Each of these organizational structures gives and receives services and communications that help staff members to achieve the goals of the district. These practices have not changed for more than a century. They are part of the folklore of American society, and as such, they have assumed an arbitrary and unquestioned place in the organization of public education. This explains why administrative relationships are still characterized by a spirit of obedience to authority, and why clear and concise duties and guidelines have been assigned to staff members so they can carry out the institutional purposes of public schools.[3]

The offices of a school district are very much the way they were 100 years ago. A school board, representing community and business interests, decides what the purposes and philosophy of the schools will be. It hires the staff who will teach in the schools. It provides constantly directive leadership so that everyone knows what is and is not significant service. The responsibility for carrying out administrative tasks is delegated to superintendents, district administrators, and building principals, who form a hierarchy, or chain of command. There is little sharing of the planning, coordinating, and channeling of district-wide policy and executive authority. There is little enlightened educational administration.[4]

The content of present-day school administration needs to be systematically studied in order to discover why it is so change resistant. Such a study would focus on the entire membership of a district. Who are they, and what are their formal and informal roles and functions? What programs are they involved in, and what are their primary and secondary responsibilities? Why have these programs been initiated, and how do they meet the needs and concerns of the district and community? How are their efforts publicized and interpreted by others? How do parents and community agencies respond to the efforts of their neighborhood schools? Where are the buildings and district offices located, and why were these sites chosen? Who has the authority and power to decide such matters? And finally, who provides the district with the funds and resources it needs to carry out its educational functions?

The administrative duties of districts are complex and diverse; the content of such activities is usually the responsibility of licensed supervisors. They decide who will be employed, in what capacity they will work, and whether or not they will have any authority outside their cellular classrooms and offices. They also decide how present-day practices will be described to community and parent groups, and they decide how financial support will be distributed in their districts. These conditions give staff a lot of power and autonomy inside their classrooms and offices, as has been noted, but outside of these classrooms they are relatively powerless. They have little to say about how many children they will serve at any one time. Thus high school counselors, for example, are often assigned 700 students, and secondary teachers may instruct 200 students on any given school day. Administration, in the traditional setting, works for the teachers and counselors, helping them to secure the materials they need in order to teach large numbers of students. It communicates with staff by pouring forth a torrent of memos, reports, and directives. However, the bureaucracy is usually unable to receive effective messages from teachers and counselors who are working directly with children. When it does receive such messages, it is often unable or unwilling to respond meaningfully.

DEMOCRATIC ADMINISTRATION

The alternative to tradition-bound administration is a communication system that is basically service-oriented and democratic in its values and procedures.[5] To develop such structures, it is necessary to train both staff members and supervisors: both need to learn to accept the responsibilities and duties of democratic administration. Most teachers and administrators support the idea of democratic administration, but few seem willing or able to put such ideas into practice; few staff members seem willing to move out of their classrooms and offices to accept the added burdens such administrative structures demand. The functioning of enlightened administration depends upon the disposition of staff: they must be willing and able to involve themselves in the planning and carrying through of the school's goals and programs. This method of administration should not be used with staff who are not ready for such added responsibilities. It is a way of administering schools that needs to be developed slowly in most instances.

Because authoritarianism is so prevalent in our schools, the usual reaction of staff when introduced to democratic governance is that it is impractical.[6] "We don't have the time!" some staff will say. Others will respond angrily, noting that administrators are paid a lot of money to make decisions. "Why don't they do their jobs and let us do ours?"

Many teachers have little patience or experience with democratic methods, especially when they are coupled with a heavy emphasis on interpersonal relations. In such instances, the skillful supervisor begins by providing staff with leadership they can appreciate. Then slowly, as her relationships with staff become more friendly and open, she introduces new ways of doing things, which should be part of the teachers' responsibilities as co-professionals in the school organization. This usually happens after she has developed a high level of trust; it comes as staff learn to work together in groups and committees and become interested in, and capable of, functioning in more conscious and effective ways.

The structure of present-day school organizations is a result of the needs of industrial society and our own unique history. It is not a fixed and immutable condition, although these structures have resisted change for many generations. They should be thought of as social processes that change according to the needs and concerns of those who operate and control the schools. They are part of a social movement that has set goals for teachers and students without asking them for their input, and adopted organizational hierarchies without considering the alienation they engender in staff, supervisors, and students. Moreover, it has evaluated the outcomes of schooling by relying too heavily on fact-dominated curriculums and examinations. The focus of administrators has been on ordering and controlling individuals inside the building rather than on improving the social, educational, and emotional relationships that develop between children and adults in schools.

Obviously, many teachers, counselors, and parents have a lot of experience with arbitrary administration. That is one reason why change has been so difficult to achieve. School administration needs to abandon these practices; it needs to adopt new organizational designs that encourage a constant communication flow back and forth between supervisors, teachers, and students.

To democratize administrative processes, principals must give up the familiar "chain of command" model of governance in favor of more circular models. Only then can they clarify the purposes of democratic administration for staff. Only then can they release the dynamic energies of staff and use the involvement and expertise of staff to achieve successful joint undertakings.

Cooperative efforts are often absent in today's schools. Initiating and carrying out new plans and policies is always dependent upon the good will and support of staff, but seldom, if ever, do staff participate in the initiation phase. When democratic programs are arbitrarily determined, teachers and counselors usually give them lip service while subverting and resisting them whenever they can. Plans that are cooperatively arrived at and implemented are usually more difficult to achieve but more successful in the long run.

Administrative and staff needs constantly change, according to the ways in which staff and students interact with each other. All teachers, counselors, and administrators are involved in the exercise of control over students. This is one of their most important tasks: to control the students' movements, to make sure that children are assigned to locations according to schedules and timetables. Only exceptional supervisors try to help staff and students free themselves from these constraints; only skillful supervisors use group processes and a knowledge of Ego Psychology to evoke consensual and cooperative behavior from staff members and students.

Much of the planning of districts and schools is done by administrators, without much consultation from those who are most affected by their plans. Cooperative planning at any level is rare. There is little pooling of ideas about how classes and guidance offices can be improved, little proactive planning. The programs that are adopted often originate in the minds of politicians, board members, or administrators who are far removed from the classrooms and guidance centers where staff members and students meet regularly. When a policy or curriculum change is agreed upon, the staff is responsible for carrying it out, no matter how they feel about it. Therefore it is not surprising that many efforts to improve schools meet with resistance. Staff are asked to put into practice approaches that are often not suitable for their particular situations.

The possibility of employing more democratic means of administration seems less than promising in today's schools, but it would reflect what research and industrial experiences have taught us: such approaches make people more productive and committed to their work, over the long run. They make people feel wanted. If supervisors could get their staff to participate in planning and policy making, it would be easier to gain support for new programs. Staff would accept responsibility for implementing innovations; they would come to see and understand budgetary problems and other difficulties that affect their everyday working conditions.

Democratic administration is usually superior to authoritarianism, as the following example makes clear.

Report #1: Junior High School #145

An important variable in the decision making processes of this urban junior high school is the personality of the principal. It reflects the needs of the authoritarian system we work in, which values directive leadership and obedience. Toward subordinates, Mr. Knott, the principal, exhibits attitudes of dominance and authority. He is the principal, the final arbiter of staff competence and behavior. He often controls his administrative staff by withholding information about his preferred procedures and practices.

Ted Braun, one of the assistant principals, is a frightened man. Even though he looks the part of an administrator, he is aware of his dependence on the principal's good will; he is also aware of the extreme disorder on the upper floors of the building. Although second in command and in constant touch with the "boss," he exercises little control over the affairs of the school. He prefers to wait until he is sure "which way the wind is blowing" before offering his ideas and opinions. He told me this himself.

I've observed him at recent meetings. Seldom do I remember him in postures of independence or initiative. When important issues arise, Mr. Knott usually turns to his insiders for advice and consent. These are old friends and "yes" men who have been with him from the beginning. They have taken over many of the positions of power and influence. Teachers, counselors, administrators, and students can be moved across the large building to new places; habits and old ways of doing things can be disrupted and new skills demanded in unknown and stressful situations.

With these insiders and administrative staff waiting to see "which way the wind will blow," I am often left as the only person who is willing to communicate distasteful news to the chief. He, in turn, feels that I am an alarmist and a troublemaker, as though the trouble I report is trouble I have somehow created. How is it I see such gloom where others see only progress and success? What is behind my behavior? Am I trying to discredit the principal and his leadership? Mr. Knott sees his school as a ship at sea, beset by dangers. My questioning of practices seems to be an act of mutiny in his eyes. We are either for or against him, he has told us many times.

"Mr. Rothstein is unhappy again. Things are not going well on the fourth floor. He feels we should reallocate our resources. Perhaps send some of you up there. Let's discuss this one more time, and then I don't want to hear about it again." Mr. Knott leaned his hands on the conference table and waited for the discussion to begin.

The six assistant principals sat in silence waiting to see "which way the wind would blow." Several insiders finally took the lead. Apparently they knew where the principal stood on this matter. Everyone was aware of the problem. But each speaker stressed that the school was larger than one floor. Operations would be hampered if administrative personnel were shifted. Who would supervise the lunchrooms? The emergency desk? Who would attend to parents and visitors? Who would complete the reports for the district? After more of this kind of talk, the cabinet agreed to send an assistant dean to work in the office on the fourth floor. As for improving the quality of instruction, that would have to wait until the teachers became more experienced.

I was the only one who talked about improving the order and instruction in the class-rooms where our untrained and inexperienced staff were working without success. The others were more concerned with other parts of the building. They were worried about losing their jobs if the community learned just how ineffective the school was in educating their children.

Toward the end of this meeting, Mr. Knott brought up another matter. "My information is that teachers are talking to parents. Listen to me! I want this stopped! Do you understand? I don't want these young snots showing how stupid and incompetent they really are! If a parent gets past the first floor security, I want the teacher to escort that person to the nearest assistant principal's office. Do you hear me? The nearest assistant principal's office! That's why we have them on each floor!"

There was some movement around the table after these remarks. Some of the insiders wanted to know how teachers could be stopped from talking to children's parents. Ted Braun felt we couldn't enforce such a rule. Community members were being sent into the school daily. If they were restricted in their communications with staff, they would surely report that to others in the community and district office. Knott listened with his head between his hand and his eyes staring downward. "Let me say it again. I am the principal in this school! I am the principal! I am responsible for everything that goes on here. And I'm giving an order! I don't want teachers talking to anyone, period! I want it stopped!" Glances fell away from one another around the table. The members of the cabinet sat silently waiting for the anger to subside, for the humiliation to end.

"I was only trying to give you my best input," Ted Braun persisted.

"I know what you were doing and I want it stopped! Don't think, Mr. Braun! Just do as I say!" Knott glared at Ted. The others cast their eyes downward. With little protest, the meeting was ended. Ted was in shock. "I only wanted to alert him." With the loud cries of the upper floors ringing in our ears, we departed for our various stations.[7]

This report describes the arbitrary nature of decision making in an urban junior high school. The principal in this meeting functioned as a boss or chairman of the board; his subordinates deferred to his authority and the power of his personality. Participation reflected a person's closeness to the school leader. Those who were insiders spoke out, while the untenured assistant principals waited to see where the principal stood. The occasion, an administrative staff meeting, depended upon the presence and participation of the principal. He was the important person without whom the meeting could not begin. Most of the staff did not participate in the discussions about whether teachers should be permitted to talk to parents about their children. Apparently, this was because important information had been withheld from them. The personal relationships of the acting administrators with the principal tended to exclude the licensed personnel from social gatherings during which policy matters were discussed. They forced outsiders to respond in confused and uncertain ways because they did not know "which way the wind was blowing."

Behaviors of passivity and fear were reinforced by the principal's tendency to shout at subordinates and to use sarcasm as a weapon to humiliate and control them. This transformed the supposedly rational structures of the junior high school organization into a power system that was ruled by the arbitrary personality of a principal who was himself under fire from the community and district office.

In this meeting, Mr. Knott unilaterally decided to forbid conversations between his teachers and the parents of ghetto school children. The nature of this school assured him that these rules would not be reviewed from above or questioned openly by others. After all, the ineffectiveness of the inexperienced staff was observable. They were unable to maintain order or engage the interest and attention of their students. Therefore they could not construct situations that could be construed as learning occasions. They could not command the respect and authority that typified the normal student-teacher relationship. Their legitimacy rested upon their supposed expertise in the educational sciences and their appointment to the teaching position. Another important criterion of teacher legitimacy was student willingness to accept staff's right to decide things in the classrooms. However the conditions in this inner-city school forced many teachers to assume a purely custodial stance since they could not maintain order or teach the children effectively.

The principal's desire to protect his inexperienced staff from the anger of the community was understandable. But it was only by seeing the decision making processes that outsiders could understand the arbitrary power that transposed the structure of impersonal rules and regulations into an authoritarian, personalized power system.[8]

THE STRUCTURE OF DEMOCRATIC ADMINISTRATION

The democratic way of doing things is a reasonable alternative to present-day administrative practices in schools. This democratic approach depends upon group structures: the formal group (the principal and his staff) is the primary mechanism that activates such cooperative ventures. The administrator, with help from committees of staff members, carries out the planning and operation of day-to-day activities, many times in ways that are determined by the problems of the individual school. Teachers and counselors are usually involved in work in their own classrooms and offices, but now they are also asked to be a permanent part of the administrative apparatus. The first step in initiating these new procedures is forming committees that work on specific classroom problems. Later the committees can be asked to deal with floorwide or building concerns. This should not begin until each group has developed a sense of unity and cohesion by working successfully on several projects.

These formal committees become, over time, the administrative structure through which the school is administered on a democratic, or representative, basis. They become a staff council to which the different faculty groups send members who participate in, and plan, the operation of the school.

While these democratic structures may look more cumbersome and unwieldy than their authoritarian counterparts, they can be more effective and purposeful in their planning of schoolwork. Administrators, working together with their staff, need to clearly define the areas of authority that these councils have in the school. The council needs to respect the autonomy and rights of formal groups and the supervisory staff. The council is a buffer between teachers and counselors, and the administrators who have traditionally directed things in the past. Through the council, staff are taught the new philosophy of the school; they are helped to find their place in the organization's emerging democratic culture.

All faculty councils have problems of identification, and these need to be understood. A group that represents the interests and viewpoints of staff fulfills the representation function as a matter of course. But it must do more than this: it must learn to identify with the problems and concerns of administration too. Unfortunately, staff do not always know how to do this. They are in a difficult position and often unable to understand their role in the administration process. They may feel they are "selling out," or not representing staff effectively, when they sympathize with the administrator's point of view. They need to learn to help teachers and counselors see that the council exists to serve their interests and those of the school. It has no other program or agenda. It is an administrative unit whose primary purpose is to serve the staff, the administration, and the children.

It is difficult to satisfy two constituencies. Council members must be able to keep their group allegiances intact as they try to function as a representative body in the school. Such positions are difficult to maintain and need the help and guidance of the supervisor. She must help council members see the differences between these administrative meetings and those they participate in with formal and influence groups.

The supervisor should make every effort to see that the faculty council functions as a constant source of communications. If the council is given real responsibilities, if it is made a functioning part of the administrative process, it will provide the administration with new perspectives and strengths.

Simple techniques can help here. There is the method of careful planning with newly elected representatives. In the first meetings the administrator should clearly define the council's responsibilities and authority as they have been agreed upon in an earlier session; she should provide staff with the resources they need to carry out their decisions. The purposes, procedures, and ground rules for the council should be thrashed out again and agreed upon before work begins.

The council is not a formal or influence group. Rather it is a link that connects the interests and concerns of many groups. To make the council function well, the administrator uses her knowledge and understanding of individual teachers and school groups; she uses her skills and insights to analyze group and social processes that affect the behavior and beliefs of staff members. The first meetings often deal with the relations between groups of staff that are represented on the council, for example, grade-level groupings, friendship formations, and interest groups. This business comes before the personal needs of members because the council is primarily the organ of formal and influence groups; it is a representative body. Council meetings seek to develop mutually satisfying goals and ways of accomplishing these goals. Later, they will need to deal with the problems individuals are having as they work together on the council. Usually, in educational administration, the primary concern is the interpersonal relationships of staff members and administrators. In this instance, however, this concern is subordinated to the task of developing friendly and cooperative relations between groups of staff members.

One important way the council fulfills its functions is through the committees it forms to deal with ongoing concerns. These committees often become permanent or standing bodies; they provide veterans and newcomers with good training as teachers move out of their isolated groups and into the arena of administration. Almost every school has a calendar of events which call for some planning and activity. It is a good idea to assign different council members to tasks during the school year and to involve as many faculty as possible in the planning and carrying out of administrative schoolwide functions. Important events give staff an opportunity to bond with their students and to become more a part of the school. The significance of these committees is related to the added prestige staff experience as they develop power and autonomy outside their work rooms. The committees are in charge of holiday celebrations, orientations and opening day schedules.

Thus a process is set in motion that highly values cooperative efforts and the sharing process. The beliefs and values that teachers and counselors hold in common bind them together, while differences are treated with respectful consideration by all members of the council. Each influence or formal group has some of its members on the council; each learns to accept and appreciate the other through its work on this intergroup administrative unit. The task of the supervisor in this process is twofold: she must help council members represent their constituencies effectively, and she must encourage them to engage as many members of their influence group as possible in the activities of the council. Rewards and commendations should go to the formal groups themselves, not to individual staff members.

The council should also develop permanent and ad hoc committees. These committees should plan and offer advice on personnel matters, budgetary problems, building maintenance, curriculum planning, and staff development. Ad hoc committees usually are formed to study problems that need clearer definition or that can be dealt with in a reasonably short period of time. Such groups often come into being when a member of the council, acting on behalf of staff, expresses concern about an activity or school problem. Members of these committees should be teachers or counselors who know something about the school and community they are trying to serve. When special expertise is required, staff members with these skills should be asked to volunteer. Later, representatives from parent and community groups can be asked to bring their points of view into the deliberations of the council and its committees. Administration would then operate through a representative structure that emphasized democratic values.

A school has to help teachers and counselors break out of their cellular isolation so they can function well in a democratically administered school.[9] A school without structures that encourage staff to participate in the running of the building is tradition-bound and change-resistant. Unfortunately, supervisors do not always see the need for change. They want to keep things the way they are. Staff are also often reluctant to change the way things are done in their school. They may feel they are already overworked and underpaid; they may believe they will not be given any meaningful authority.

Supervisors need to make a deliberate and sustained effort to provide staff members with channels and structures that encourage schoolwide participation and involvement. They need to do this even when their first efforts are met with hostility and suspicion. They should understand that it will take time before teachers and counselors come to see them as concerned, helpful co-professionals.

DEMOCRATIC ADMINISTRATION AND PLANNING

Council committees make specific and general plans for the school. Specific plans are carried out after they have been approved by the faculty council. Policy matters and schoolwide decisions are usually dealt with by the council as a whole.

The objectives of program planning sessions are broad: to coordinate specific and general program plans, avoid duplication, and assure staff of their right to carry out programs they develop. The faculty council should have standing members from each grade and from special curricular groups. The committees can be chosen from council members, or from other teachers and counselors who are willing to serve. Later, special interest groups will want to have their say. Parents, students, and community groups may seek some role on the council once they see it is an effective administrative force.

The functions of the council should be spelled out: to explore and clarify the special tasks of the school in light of its legally stated purposes; to systematically examine the existing methods and curriculum to see whether they meet the needs of students and the goals of the school; to study the special needs of the community to improve the school's services; to formulate plans for school improvement based on the information developed in committee work; and finally, to periodically evaluate council efforts.

While introducing the new methods of administration, it is important to maintain the quality of education. Democratic planning and evaluation is difficult to administer. However, the effort of co-professionals to constantly study and evaluate their work is obviously worthwhile and needed. There is simply no better way to administer a school than this: to work with teachers and counselors rather than for them, and to use staff energies and insights to build a cohesive, co-operative effort that benefits children. Each formal group and each influence group needs to develop its knowledge and skills, so it can take on the duties and privileges of a democratic administration.

PROGRAM PLANNING

Program planning meetings are often called by council committees or faculty groups that want to examine what they are doing in their classrooms and how they can make improvements. The group is sometimes autonomous, as are most informal grade-oriented committees. Program planning committees may report their findings to the council without seeking its assent or approval. After all, their members are the experts, the ones who are dealing with students every day. Sometimes, however, their plan may go against the specific policies or guidelines of the school or demand things from faculty that are prohibited by union contracts. Therefore the council should listen carefully to suggestions for change. What are the problems? What solutions are being suggested? How will they affect different groups of teachers, counselors, and students? Are they workable given the present conditions? Some committees of the council may examine the unmet needs of parents and community groups, suggesting ways for improving communication and services to these groups.

Each council representative asks her influence group to formulate ideas for solving problems or developing new programs. Then the council discusses the group reports and suggestions. Are they in harmony with the general curriculum and learning goals of the school? What changes must be made in the structure or stated purposes of the school? How many staff and paraprofessionals will be needed? How many students will be involved? What kinds of materials will be needed? The final plan is agreed upon by the council and sent to executive committees, which help provide staff with the equipment and materials they will need. Copies of the final report are also sent to the administrator so she can plan her role in the new program. Committees concerned with personnel matters may suggest staff for a new program who are particularly skilled in certain areas or in solving interpersonal problems. In this way, problems and new programs become the responsibility and concern of many; many staff members become part of the implementation process and participate in the frequent evaluation sessions that monitor the progress of school improvement efforts. Thus, the entire school community, not just one or two people, is involved in the education process.

VOLUNTEERS AND PARAPROFESSIONALS

Time must be set aside during the school day so that teachers and counselors can participate in council meetings. Because the purposes of democratic administration are to provide staff with a chance to involve themselves in schoolwide planning, paraprofessionals and volunteers have an important role to play.

How should paraprofessionals and volunteers be used? They should be given work that they can do well: work that fits their individual backgrounds, knowledge, and training. At first, the assignments should be clearly defined; they should fit the larger plans of the classroom. Later, the administrative staff can provide volunteers, paraprofessionals, and others with in-service training and staff development seminars.

To recruit paraprofessionals and volunteers, a school must publicize the positions available. A call for volunteers should include information about the kinds of services volunteers will perform and the opportunities that exist for advancement.

An effective program of recruitment ought to consider the following: (1) it should operate all through the school year, even though actual hiring may be limited to specific periods of time; and (2) it should encourage applicants to apply whenever they express an interest. Administrators should ask staff for clearly defined job descriptions that spell out in detail what volunteers and paraprofessionals will be doing in the classroom or guidance office. Such job descriptions should include a statement of duties and areas of responsibility; they should specify what personal and educational training aides will need. How much time will they have to put in each day? Will they be asked to participate in in-service training before they begin their work? In some instances, seminars may be a requirement before an aide can begin to serve in the school. When and where will such training be given, and by whom?

Leaders who want to develop a democratic administration need to seek out and use paraprofessionals and volunteers effectively. Enlightened practice requires frequent meetings, conferences, staff development seminars, and planning sessions. Only by using paraprofessionals and volunteers can a school meet the needs of hundreds of children and staff members and free teachers and counselors from custodial duties.

Paraprofessionals and volunteers can help in many ways. With the proper training, they can act as auxiliary teachers. They can help teachers to communicate with children who have language disabilities or speak a foreign language in their homes. Some members of district boards of education may be volunteers. Special events committees often look for guidance and support from parents and community agencies. Usually these advisory persons are asked for their thoughts and opinions about program objectives that have already been adopted. Then that advice can be accepted or not by the committees or administrators who have been given the authority and responsibility for deciding on, and carrying out, new programs. Paraprofessionals and volunteers have to work within the framework of policies and educational programs adopted by the administrative apparatus of the school.

Leaders who succeed in introducing democratic administration into their schools need to recruit and train volunteers and paraprofessionals from the community they serve. Should the skillful supervisor be concerned with the kind of supervision new volunteers might reasonably expect? Who will be their mentors, their guides? Recruitment committees will have to answer these questions and more; they will have to match volunteers to particular jobs and teachers based on the information they gather in interviews and seminars. They will have to receive feedback from staff as well as evaluation reports from them. How is the volunteer or paraprofessional doing and what is the meaning of his schoolwork for him, for staff, and for the students? The following is a report on a paraprofessional training program, which was implemented in a junior high school in southern California:

Report #2: Effects of Open Communication Systems on Aides

The commitment to conference everyone in the reading center had an unexpected effect. People are beginning to find out more about each other. Today, teachers reported that aides and volunteers felt excluded and rejected by teachers. They are being asked to do all the dirty work and seldom get a chance to work with the children one-on-one. Their aspirations are being ignored. They want to do more professional, challenging work; some are thinking of becoming teachers themselves. But none of the staff seemed to know this before the weekly conference system was initiated and paraprofessionals aired their grievances. They are tired of always cleaning up after a learning period has ended.

As a result of the revelations in recent conferences, volunteers and paraprofessionals are being given more say in deciding their roles and duties with students. Needless to say, this has raised the morale. In-service training today stressed one-on-one tutoring and the use of audio-visual equipment in the teaching of reading.

Children are responding differently to the aides and paraprofessionals. They are coming to see them as "helpers who really care," as one of the youngsters phrased it. Even so, much remains to be done. Some progress is being made in breaking the barriers between staff and their aides. But the gap between the black and brown paraprofessionals and the white staff needs more attention and work. Today, at a teacher's conference, several staff admitted they never see black or brown people in their social lives outside the school. They only come into contact with them at school, and their views are colored by their educational problems and socioeconomic condition. So a lot will have to be done with stereotypes; a lot will have to be done if teachers are going to understand and relate well to their aides and paraprofessionals.[10]

STAFF SELECTION

Two conclusions appear again and again in the findings of researchers who have studied the kinds of persons who choose education as a course of study and occupational career path: most are the lowest achieving undergraduates in their class, and they opt for education as a "last resort."[11] Therefore, administrators have to recruit persons who are willing to attend seminars and in-service and other training during their tenure in the school; they will have to find teachers and counselors who are willing and eager to upgrade their skills.

As the school's initial contact persons, administrators should help newcomers understand what is expected of them. Whatever their previous education and training, new teachers need special qualities to see them through their new, stressful circumstances. To begin with, they must be people-oriented and interested in serving the needs of the children. They must be friendly and accepting, understanding that people may do things in many different ways. They need to be sensitive to the differing values and norms that individuals bring into the school.

Recognition of the right of others to do things in their own way and respect for other people's values are two important qualities to look for in the search for good staff. Prospective candidates should also be knowledgeable about the group process and the way it influences the morale and welfare of others. Effective staff are service-oriented: they gain satisfaction by working with and through students, and they are giving persons who tend to accept and support youngsters and other staff.

Good staff somehow convey to students the goals and values of their own philosophy and that of the school. The way in which they do this determines how successful they will be. Supervisors can help staff clarify their goals and reflect on their methods. Regularly scheduled supervision meetings place newcomers in a problem solving cycle which helps them to work through their problems in the school. Staff are professionals who work with people every day; they should be given a chance to participate in training that upgrades their knowledge and skills.

The assistant principal should have a number of years of teaching experience on several grade levels if possible. Thus she will be aware of the normal development of children as they grow from childhood into adolescence. She should also have skills in problem solving and supervision. Her first contacts with new staff and aides often set the tone for their future associations. Therefore these first meetings should clearly spell out the expectations of the school and provide newcomers with concrete evidence of the administration's friendliness and acceptance.

ADMINISTRATIVE DUTIES

The enlightened educational administration approach is based on the assumption of service.[12] Supervisory staff have many duties:

1. Schools must communicate with the community they serve or they will be misunderstood and attacked by the public. In general, the administrator must perform this important task. A significant amount of information has to be gathered and disseminated if administration is to make intelligent decisions based upon the needs of the community. After all, the school is made up of children who live in the surrounding neighborhood and have the same values and norms as their families and friends. Different communities have different personalities. If they are homogeneous in their

socioeconomic makeup, communities will have specific demands for their schools. Learning more about the families and people in the community is an important part of the school administrator's job.

2. The supervisor also has responsibilities. She should advise and participate in faculty councils, helping their members understand and involve themselves in the administration of the school. She is also responsible for school programs and policy decisions. She is responsible for the administration and supervision of instruction and serves as a resource person for teachers and faculty committees. For teachers and counselors who are having discipline or instructional problems, she provides individual and group conferences to help them identify and resolve their difficulties.

3. Administrators cannot accomplish all these tasks by themselves. They have to delegate, organize, and give responsibility to teachers and counselors who participate in the democratic operation of the school. With the responsibility for doing a particular task must come authority to take effective action and an accountability to the administration which empowers staff to act on its behalf. When the administrator gives staff the responsibility for certain areas of administration, she assumes the duty of supervising and coordinating their efforts and of helping staff to function as well as they can. She uses conferences, group meetings, seminars, and in-service training sessions to support and encourage teachers and counselors to become more conscious and more responsive to children.

4. Faculty want to work in rewarding professional environments. The administrator is responsible for the school climate and the morale of her staff; she is responsible for the educational and emotional relationships that develop in the school. She helps staff do their work, according to their own individual personalities and styles, within the framework of democratic educational practice. However, the school leader is not responsible for the emotional development of staff. She is only responsible for establishing a co-professional relationship with staff that provides an environment which allows them to grow and develop. She should help faculty improve their skills while teaching new faculty members to put into practice the knowledge and skills they already possess.

5. People are motivated best when they participate in the decision making process. Therefore administrators should seek to involve staff in the administration of the school whenever possible. How will they retain control over staff's actions? The controls will come from peer groups, common values and norms, and the demands of the community and the work itself. The administrator cannot completely control the behavior of staff. She can only structure situations so that the teaching and guidance activities are done with empathy and skill, so that teachers, counselors, and supervisors benefit from their efforts to reach common goals.

SUMMARY

The "how-to" of the communication system in democratic administration is learned in weekly staff conferences. These conferences are regularly scheduled meetings with teachers, counselors, and aides, which are held during the school day. Their length is often determined by their content and the time constraints of the school. These meetings provide supervisors and staff with a chance to learn more about one another. What problems need to be discussed? What plans? What kinds of knowledge and skills will be needed to carry out the programs teachers and counselors have agreed upon? These are some of the questions which may be discussed during such meetings.

During weekly staff conferences, administrators, faculty, and aides can jointly evaluate how they are doing during the school term. The schedules of staff are sometimes changed in order to meet new conditions and situations. The resources and allocations are also discussed, and decisions are made about new purchases of educational materials.

Staff conferences are opportunities for staff and aides to learn about the needs of students; they are organizational structures which inform participants of the needs of other staff members who are working with them to provide better learning situations for children. In these staff conferences, the concerns of the community are brought into the open where they can be analyzed and better understood. Classroom and guidance activities of staff are also constantly scrutinized in these conference in order to better understand the unmet needs of students, teachers, and counselors.

The staff conference is an important part of administration and affects the climate, morale, and problem solving abilities of staff members and students. It asks staff to clarify their own purposes and behavior and those of the administration in which they serve; it asks them to commit themselves to common goals and purposes. This commitment is made possible through the role teachers, counselors, and aides play in the school. Each individual is provided many opportunities to express their opinions, thoughts, and feelings. This is done in an atmosphere of acceptance and mutual regard, where problems are identified and resolved in group meetings and individual conferences. The morale of staff and aides is high in these kinds of settings because of the mutual feelings of support and confidence they generate.

In democratic administrations, staff conferences, unlike those in authoritarian schools, are meetings which use the group process to build relationships between staff members; they are communication channels. In addition, they help staff and administration develop better relationships and work habits.

Here again, the role of the administrator is one of facilitation, inquiry, and supervision. The progress of a group conference should not be held back because of the behavior of aggressive individuals; quiet teachers, counselors, and aides should be encouraged to have their say. It is the administrator's duty to intervene in the process to assure that dominant persons do not simply "walk over" introspective members, and that shy individuals are given an opportunity to express themselves. It is her responsibility to establish relationships with each staff member with whom she works. She is a member of the group, but she is also the supervisor. She is separate and apart from them because of the authority of her official position. Her remarks and opinions have a greater impact than those of others because of the rank and status which goes with her position. Therefore a school leader's work is mostly an enabling task: she serves staff best by encouraging them to involve themselves in the administrative processes of the school.

Administrators who want to use democratic staff conferences should be aware that some teachers and counselors will need help in order to participate constructively. Newcomers and older faculty may find it hard to accept their administrators as inquiring, facilitating group leaders. They may demand that the supervisor provide them with direction and advice. Others may resist because of their own lack of self-confidence; they may not take an active part because they are afraid they will be rejected once they reveal too much about themselves. Sometimes these problems can be dealt with most effectively in individual meetings where the fears, anxieties, and anger of teachers, counselors, and aides can be expressed more openly.

Occasionally, seminars about specific educational matters can be held in the school. Both supervisors and staff should agree on the purpose of seminars and the choice of teachers, or team leaders to organize them. The discussion of problems and conflicts sometimes requires the knowledge and expertise of persons who are outside the school's organization. For newcomers, training courses can be established to familiarize them with the methods and procedures of the school. The content of such orientations will depend upon the knowledge, skills, and background of participants.

Supervisors are constantly using different knowledge and skills to help staff improve their performance through (1) weekly supervision meetings; (2) intervention strategies that affect the way that people interact in conferences; (3) application of insights about the group process to the problems and concerns of staff; (4) maintenance of records on staff progress; (5) scheduling of individual and group meetings which help staff reflect upon their behavior and goals; (6) planning for the allocation of materials and equipment; and (7) communications with community agencies that helps them understand and support the school's policies and programs.

As administrators, supervisors are asked to lead others and to enable them to take over the leadership function in their areas of expertise. Staff are co-professionals—they are supposed to make informed decisions about the children they serve with the help and guidance of other faculty.

Democratic administration, then, is a way of communicating with staff. It is a method of supervision and problem solving which uses conferences to help staff analyze and function in more conscious, empathetic ways and work toward common educational goals. These goals have individual and group aspects: they help staff to move out of their cellular isolation and enable them to become more effective social beings; they encourage groups of staff to participate actively in the running of the school.

ACTIVITIES

1. Analyze the climate in your school. Then observe and analyze the administrative processes used there. What type of communication patterns exist? How much authority

do teachers have outside their classrooms? How satisfied are they with the present administrative system? How dissatisfied? What could you suggest that might make administration more democratic? How would such suggestions be received by teachers? By administrators? By board members?

2. Analyze the way staff members are selected at your school. What procedures are used? How many people are involved in the selection? What are the criteria? What problems develop once teachers have been hired and begin to do the work? How satisfied are new teachers with the help they get? How satisfied are administrators? Write down three suggestions that might help your school to choose better staff members.

NOTES

1. F. Lutz and C. Mertz, *The Politics of School/Community Relations* (New York: Teachers College Press, 1992); Andrew W. Halpin, *Theory and Research in Administration* (New York: MacMillan Company, 1972), pp. 174–175.

2. Stanley W. Rothstein, *Schools and Society: New Perspectives in American Education* (Englewood Cliffs, N.J.: Prentice-Hall, 1996), pp. 1–13; Stanley W. Rothstein, "Orientations: First Impressions in an Urban Junior High School," *Urban Education*, Vol. 14, No. 1 (April 1971); Stanley W. Rothstein, "The Socialization of the School Administrator," *Private School Quarterly* (Spring 1983), pp. 52–60.

3. Stanley W. Rothstein, *Schooling the Poor: A Social Inquiry into the American Educational Experience* (Westport, Conn.: Bergin & Garvey, 1994), pp. 200–204.

4. Willard Waller, "What Teaching Does to Teachers," in M. Stein, A. Vidich, and S. White (eds.), *Identity and Anxiety* (Glencoe, Ill.: Free Press, 1962); Thomas J. Sergiovanni and Robert J. Starratt, *Supervision: Human Perspectives* (New York: McGraw-Hill, 1988).

5. Educational Policies Commission, *The Structure and Administration of Education in American Democracy* (Washington, D.C.: National Education Association, 1938), pp. 67–68; J. A. Stepsis, "Structure as an Integrative Concept in Management: Theory and Practice," in John E. Jones and J. William Pfeiffer (eds.), *The 1977 Annual Handbook for Group Facilitators* (La Jolla, Calif.: University Associates Press, 1977), pp. 169–179; Alfred Marrow, David Bowers, and Stanley Seashore, *Management by Partition* (New York: Harper and Row, 1967).

6. Stanley William Rothstein, "The Ethics of Coercion," *Urban Education*, Vol. XXII, No. 1 (April 1987), pp. 53–72.

7. R. Wynn and C. Guditus, *Team Management: Leadership by Consensus* (Columbus, Ohio: Charles E. Merrill Publishing Company, 1984), pp. 112–120.

8. From my field notes.

9. Ivan Steiner, *Group Process and Productivity* (New York: Academic Press, 1972), p. 176; C. R. Bell, *Managers as Mentors: Building Partnerships for Learning* (San Francisco: Pfeiffer, 1996).

10. From my field notes.

11. R. Rebore, *Personnel Administration in Education* (Englewood Cliffs, N.J.: Prentice-Hall, 1984), pp. 79–83.

12. Wynn and Guditus, *Team Management*, pp. 101–120.

8

Making Leadership Choices

An administrator must make choices soon after she is appointed to her position. She must decide what kind of person she wants to be, what kind of leadership she is going to provide for staff members and students. How can she escape the authoritarian mold of traditional schools? How can she choose the right style of leadership for this particular school?

In making such decisions, she would be wise to remember that learning is a process, and so is the evolution of leadership styles in particular situations. *What kind of leadership has staff experienced in the past? How did they like it? What kinds of relationships did they have with the previous supervisor? Do they want direction or are they more independent-minded?* In establishing a democratic administration, the administrator needs to begin where staff are in their social and educational development. Her decisions need to take into consideration the feelings and concerns of staff. Only then can she learn what she needs to know to be more effective. Only when she understands the learning cycle can she provide staff with the kinds of behavior they need and want. Later, as her relationships develop, she can begin the process of freeing staff from their isolation and traditional ways of doing things. She can establish friendships that are supported by acceptance and mutual respect rather than evaluation and dependency. She can strengthen the democratic ideas and values which are a part of the larger culture.

The way an administrator reacts to others determines whether she will be isolated and alone, or part of a cooperative group. It will influence the way she sees things and how well informed she is about what is happening in the school. The way the administrator behaves will deeply affect the kind of person she becomes at work and in her personal life.

If she chooses to behave in traditional ways, she will find herself persuading and directing others, cajoling them, forcing them to do things they may not want to do. She will teach them to attend and obey. This way of leading creates a great deal of confusion among staff. She may become paranoid, constantly on guard against any dissent or disagreement. She may see threats to her authority and leadership where none exist. According to Chris Argyris, these types of managers have a low opinion of the people who work for them. They see subordinates as lazy, purposeless persons who cannot behave in an intelligent and resourceful manner.[1]

Choosing "bossism" as a way of leading will also affect the administrator in other ways. She will come to see herself as the responsible person who must decide everything because she is legally charged to do so. She is the one who must enforce the rules and regulations. She must make sure curriculum guidelines are followed. She is the lonely one who must lead others who are untrustworthy and ungrateful.

An administrator who believes in "bossism" must hide deficiencies and doubts, lest they make her more vulnerable. She must withhold information, so that others will be dependent on her judgment and expertise. The personal front that she presents may differ at first from her inner feelings. But later, the two may come together. She may become a person who is feared and disliked, or she may develop a reputation as an angry, unreliable person. Such a reputation seems to be the fate of many school administrators today.

There is, then, the problem of becoming devious in one's statements and behavior. There is the added problem of becoming lonely and alone in a school crowded with people. Therefore every administrator has a real and pressing interest in breaking the mold of directive leadership. Every administrator has a stake in developing more friendly and accepting school climates. Only by consciously making these choices can administrators communicate well with teachers and counselors. Only then can they develop mental attitudes that foster their own psychological health and well-being. Staff must have environments that encourage them to say and do what they think is right. They need to be in a climate which allows them to be themselves, without being afraid of rejection or ridicule. Staff need to establish close relationships with others around them, and they need to have the opportunity to know these others honestly and without fear.

Listening to others is an essential skill, as is the language of acceptance as it is applied, clearing her mind of what she wants to say, what she feels and thinks so she can listen more attentively. The language of acceptance leads to more accurate interpretations of what others are saying. It helps the supervisor see the world through the eyes of significant others. It also makes her more sensitive to the responses and behavior of the staff.

SCHOOL CLIMATES

The way a supervisor administers her school will affect how people respond to one another. Therefore choosing a leadership style is important in determining how friendly and effective staff and students will be. The coercive, arbitrary leadership of traditional administration confuses everyone and reduces the level of communication between people. It makes it more difficult for administrators to know what is happening. Teachers and counselors learn to obey and attend; they seldom initiate anything. They try to make things sound a little better than they are when asked about their problems. They tend to be unaware of the depths of anger and resentment they feel toward administrators who keep them dependent and anxious. Furthermore, supervisors become suspicious of those who disagree with them, while staff look down on those among their number who try to win the administrator's favor.

Leaders who use the power of their office to force staff to do things their way are "lonely at the top." They work in an unfriendly, tense climate in which their own weaknesses confound their relationships with others. They have few friends. In addition, they seldom have the information they need to identify and resolve serious problems. Staff are careful in their interactions because they know their mistakes will become the subject of official evaluations.

Relationships are shallow and formal at best. Staff see administrators as manipulative types who don't remember what it is like to work with children.

The drawbacks to directive leadership are many: school problems are decided without sufficient input or insight; staff become more closed and distant in their communications; and staff are frustrated by their lack of empowerment. When staff must compete for good evaluations and the acceptance of the supervisor, relationships with other staff are less friendly and cooperative. Staff members are less willing to involve themselves. This inevitably leads to less efficient and less informed leadership. Schools are organized to reflect the authoritarian ethos of the work place.

There are workers and bosses. There are those who direct and decide and those who obey and listen. But they seldom reflect the democratic values of our society. They do not provide teachers, counselors, or students with the basic civil rights or representative government. This failure points the way we must travel: administrators must strive to establish schools that provide staff members and students with a healthy and democratic climate.

How is this to be done? How can supervisors serve these needs? This book attempts to answer such questions. A school needs to serve the goals of everyone in the building. Therefore administrators should seek ways of involving people. They should establish structures that are capable of reacting to new times, situations, and relationships. Whenever possible, problems will have to be identified and resolved by those who are most closely linked to them. This should be done with the help and assistance of the administrator. She needs to make people aware of the deeper significance of their behavior and feelings as they affect the schooling process.

ADMINISTRATORS AND TEACHERS

More and more, staff are losing respect for their supervisors. As they become more experienced and tenured, teachers and counselors tend to dismiss their administrators as ineffective and unsupportive. This affects the performance and climate within which children learn and may hurt their educational performance.

Why does this happen? One reason seems to be the impersonal behavior that exists in so many schools today. A second is overcrowding. Moreover, the behavior of administrators has been overly evaluative and punitive; they have not shown an understanding of how staff learn to do their work better. Administrators have been avoided or ignored because they are too judgmental and inspection minded. ("My supervisor? He's wonderful! I never see him! He leaves me alone and I leave him alone. We get along just fine!")

Supervisors lose the confidence of teachers and counselors when they try to tell staff what to do; when they insist on following the letter of a rule or regulation in every circumstance. No one but the staff person knows what kind of approach will work best in a particular situation. Only she is in constant contact with the students. Therefore the wise administrator learns to be a facilitator.

Still, there are always going to be conflicts and disagreements which have to be worked out. And if supervisors involve staff in problem solving situations, they will gain two things: greater involvement and more open expressions of thoughts and feelings. Getting an administrator to accept these gains can be difficult. Most have been trained to seek consensus, no matter how it was achieved; they have been taught that discord and disagreement are tantamount to disloyalty.

Why is conflict a "gain" in organizational terms? Simmel explained this a long time ago.[2] When staff disagree, their norms, values, and beliefs come to the surface where they can be dealt with by a perceptive and skillful supervisor. Administrators come to see that different individuals have to be handled differently. Conflicts identify areas of stress and tension in the organization, places where the skillful supervisor can focus her efforts to harness the ideas and emotions of staff members in the pursuit of common goals. Therefore, conflict can be a positive development in organizational settings. It provides the supervisor with an opportunity to bring understanding and cohesion to her school.

Disagreements arise between a supervisor and staff member over how children should be taught, what they should be taught, how assignments should be made, and how students should be disciplined. Take the teacher who allows youngsters to talk in class. For many teachers today, a quiet, purposeful classroom climate has a mystical significance. It isn't important for a supervisor to understand why obedience is so important; it is essential that she realize that order and control come first when classrooms contain 36 children or more. The teacher values silence because it helps her to maintain control. It means she can direct her students to concerns she feels are important. She is unaware of how students feel when they are forced to sit in silence all day. She prefers this silence because she needs it to maintain order and control; she doesn't know how to use group processes to establish learning situations and classroom control.

Attempts by supervisors to force staff to change, or efforts to shame them, will meet with resistance. Quiet, purposeful classrooms are the sign of an effective teacher in traditional schools, as they were 200 years ago. Therefore administrators will do well to accept these views at first. They will do well to befriend such teachers and to accept their explanations of why they act as they do. Later, conferences can help teachers become more aware of the human costs of these modes of instruction.

The message a supervisor wants to communicate is one of understanding and acceptance. "I understand why silence is important to you. I accept your right to decide such things in your classroom." Given the present level of training of teachers and counselors, this is what administrators should expect when they begin to work with teachers. To make changes, the supervisor must begin the process of establishing a supportive, accepting environment. Then she can make the teacher more aware of her behavior and its effects on the children she teaches. In time, the teacher will come to see how children respond to dictatorial leadership, and she will be ready for new ways of dealing with them.

Democratic administration accepts the idea that there are many ways to do schoolwork. Supervision should not be a method for forcing everyone into a mold. If administrators use their friendships and information to do this, it is certain staff will see them in less accepting and more mistrustful ways.

Administrators will always be in the spotlight whether they like it or not. Everyone will be watching them. They will provide teachers and counselors with examples of how to respond to pressure and crises and how to react to the behavior of others. Their actions, rather than their words, will send messages to staff members and to students.

Supervisors can develop good relationships by being consistent in what they say and do. If supervisors want their staff to communicate more truthfully, they have to demonstrate their concern by being open in their own expressions and communications. If they want staff to be more accepting, they must be accepting too. If they want staff to be more reflective and conscious, they must model such behavior in their interactions with others. This is the way that democratic values can be taught most effectively.

Whatever school leaders say to their staff members often goes in one ear and out the other. Supervisors have been out of the classroom for so many years they don't understand, the teachers often say to one another. However, when these leaders establish friendly relationships and behave consistently, they improve their ability to influence the behavior of staff members.

ADMINISTRATIVE LEADERSHIP

The administrator must be the leader—she must provide her staff with an anxiety-free work climate. This means giving up the traditional desire to change and control teachers and counselors, to improve them. It means providing them with an environment that permits change if members feel the need for it. But before this can happen, supervisors and staff must overcome preconceptions developed in earlier experiences that learning is an unpleasant experience that creates embarrassment and discomfort. The supervisor needs to be patient with the confusion and ambivalence that staff members may show in new situations. Staff are sometimes confused and troubled by their new freedom and responsibility because it is so different from what they have known in the past.

What are the reasons for pursuing these new ways? Why is it important for the supervisor to have skills in human development and problem solving? Why insist on having teachers and counselors verbalize their thoughts and feelings in regular meetings? The answer is that the ego must be strengthened by constant use and development. Moreover, the learning process needs to proceed from the known to the unknown, from the simple to the complex, and from what is understood to what is problematical.

To understand the learning process as it develops in democratically administered schools, one must realize that each person has competencies and knowledge that form the start of their own learning experiences. The supervisor must begin with what is known.

The administrator must view learning as a gradual and uneven movement from what is known and understood, to new knowledge and skills, to new insights and behavior. Staff have to be ready to learn the curriculum adopted by their peers. They need to confront their future with a continuing sense of accomplishment and recognition. This also holds true for the young children they are instructing in classrooms and guidance offices.

Equal in importance to these staff development ideas is the need of staff members to learn by doing: experiential learning is best if it grows out of the needs and concerns of staff members and their students. Such learning causes everyone to become more committed to their own educational experiences and to the school which provides them with such opportunities.

Everywhere today, business and industry are looking for new and more effective ways to do their work. They are moving away from bossism and arbitrary leadership toward democratic, cooperative forms of human effort and teamwork. Therefore, there is a chance that the change-resistant schools will finally change too. This must occur if the values and traditions of our society are to prosper and survive.

NOTES

1. Chris Argyris, "Interpersonal Barriers to Decision-Making," *Harvard Business Review*, No. 40 (1966), pp. 84–97.
2. Georg Simmel, *Conflict and the Web of Group Affiliations* (Glencoe, Ill.: Free Press, 1955).

Selected Bibliography

Albrow, Martin. *Bureaucracy.* London: Macmillan, 1970.

Altenbaugh, Richard J. "Families, Children, Schools and the Workplace." In Stanley W. Rothstein (ed.), *Handbook of Schooling in Urban America.* Westport, Conn.: Greenwood Press, 1993, pp. 19–42.

———. "Italian and Mexican Responses to Schooling: Assimilation or Resistance?" In Stanley W. Rothstein (ed.), *Class, Culture and Race in American Schools: A Handbook.* Westport, Conn.: Greenwood Press, 1995, pp. 91–106.

———. *The Teacher's Voice: A Social History of Teaching in Twentieth Century America.* London: Falmer, 1992.

Anastasi, T. *Face to Face Communication.* Cambridge, Mass.: Management Center for Cambridge, 1967.

Aron, Raymond. *Main Currents in Sociological Thought, Part II: Durkheim, Pareto, Weber.* New York: Basic Books, 1967.

Argyris, Chris. "Interpersonal Barriers to Decision-Making." *Harvard Business Review,* No. 44 (1966), pp. 84–97.

———. *Management and Organizational Development.* New York: McGraw-Hill, 1971.

Banks, Olive. *The Sociology of Education.* New York: Schocken Books, 1976.

Bass, Bernard M. *Leadership, Psychology, and Organizational Behavior.* New York: Harper & Brothers, 1960.

Becher, Tony, and Stuart Maclure. *The Politics of Curriculum Change.* London: Hutchinson, 1978.

Bell, C. R. *Managers as Mentors: Building Partnerships for Learning.* San Francisco: Pfeiffer, 1996.

Bendix, Reinhard. "Bureaucracy and the Problem of Power." In Robert Merton, Asa Gray, B. Hockey, and H. Selvin (eds.), *Reader in Bureaucracy.* New York: Free Press, 1976.

———. *Max Weber: An Intellectual Portrait.* New York: Doubleday-Anchor, 1962.

———. "Max Weber's Intepretation of Conduct and History." *American Journal of Sociology*, Vol. LI (May 1946), pp. 518–526.

Benne, K. D., and P. Sheats. "Functional Roles of Group Members." In *Group Development*. Washington, D.C.: National Training Laboratories, 1961, pp. 51–59.

Bernstein, Basil. *The Structuring of Pedagogic Discourse*, Vol. IV, *Class, Codes and Control*. London: Routledge & Kegan Paul, 1990.

———. *Theoretical Studies towards a Sociology of Language*, Vol. 1, *Class, Codes and Control*. London: Routledge & Kegan Paul, 1975.

Blanck, G., and R. Blanck. *Ego Psychology: Theory and Practice*. New York: Columbia University Press, 1974.

Blau, Peter. *Bureaucracy in Modern Society*. New York: Random House, 1956.

Bolman, Lee. "Theory, Practice, and Educational Administration: Bridging Troublesome Dichotomies." *Education and Urban Society* (November 1976), pp. 67–80.

Bruhn, J. G., and A. S. Gurman. "Measuring Social Support: A Synthesis of Current Approaches." *Journal of Behavioral Medicine*, Vol. 7 (1984), pp. 151–169.

Carkhuff, R. *The Art of Helping*. Amherst, Mass.: Human Resource Development Press, 1987.

Combs, Arthur W., Donald L. Avila, and William W. Purkey. *Helping Relationships: Basic Concepts for the Helping Professions*. Boston: Allyn and Bacon, 1971.

Cormier, W. H., and L. S. Cormier. "Choice or Change: Issues of Clients and How to Work with Them." *Journal of Counseling and Human Service Professions*, Vol. 1, No. 1 (1986), pp. 88–99.

———. *Interviewing Strategies for Helpers: Fundamental Skills and Cognitive Behavioral Interventions*. Pacific Grove, Calif.: Brooks/Cole Publishing Company, 1985.

Corwin, R. G. *A Sociology of Education*. New York: Appleton-Century-Crofts, 1965.

Cuban, Larry. *How Teachers Taught: Constancy and Change in American Classrooms 1890–1980*. New York: Longman, 1984.

Cummins, John. "Empowering Minority Students: A Framework for Intervention." *Harvard Educational Review*, Vol. 56 (1966), pp. 18-36.

Darder, Antonia. *Culture and Power in the Classroom*. New York: Bergin & Garvey, 1991.

Dewey, John. *Experience and Education*. New York: Macmillan, 1938.

Driscoll, R. *Pragmatic Psychotherapy*. New York: Van Nostrand Reinhold, 1984.

Dubin, A. R., S. Pinick, and W. Youtz. *From Delinquency to Freedom*. Seattle: Special Child Publications, 1970.

Durkheim, Emile. *The Division of Labor in Society*. New York: Macmillan, 1947.

———. *Education and Society*. New York: Free Press, 1956.

———. *Education and Sociology*. Glencoe, Ill.: Free Press, 1956.

———. *Moral Education: A Study in the Theory and Application of the Sociology of Education*. Everett K. Wilson and Herman Schnurer (trans.). New York: The Free Press of Glencoe, 1961.

Eckert, P. A., N. Abeles, and R. N. Graham. "Symptom Severity, Psychotherapy Process and Outcome." *Professional Psychology: Research and Practice*, No. 19 (1988), pp. 560–564.

Egan, G. *Change Agent Skills in Helping and Human-Service Settings*. Pacific Grove, Calif.: Brooks/Cole Publishing Company, 1985.

———. *The Skilled Helper: A Systematic Approach to Effective Helping.* Pacific Grove, Calif.: Brooks/Cole Publishing Company, 1990.

Eggleston, John. *The Sociology of School Curriculum.* London: Routledge & Kegan Paul, 1977.

Ellis, A. *Overcoming Resistance: Rational-Emotive Therapy with Difficult Clients.* New York: Springer, 1985.

Emery, E. E. "Empathy: Psychoanalytic and Client-Centered." *American Psychologist,* Vol. 42 (1966), pp. 513–515.

Fiedler, F. *A Theory of Leadership Effectiveness.* New York: McGraw-Hill, 1967.

Fielder, Fred E., and Martin M. Chemers. *Leadership and Effective Management.* Glenview, Ill.: Scott, Foresman & Company, 1974.

Freire, Paulo. *The Pedagogy of the Oppressed.* New York: Seabury Press, 1970.

Freud, Sigmund. *Civilization and its Discontents.* James Strachey (trans.). New York: W. W. Norton, 1962.

———. *The Ego and the Id.* Joan Riviere (trans.). New York: W. W. Norton, 1960.

———. *Introductory Lectures on Psychoanalysis.* James Strachey (ed. and trans.). New York: W. W. Norton, 1977.

Freund, Julien. *The Sociology of Max Weber.* Mary Alford (trans.). New York: Pantheon Books, 1968.

Fuchs, Estelle. *Teachers Talk.* Garden City, N.Y.: Doubleday, 1966.

Gay, Peter. *Freud: A Life for Our Time.* New York: Doubleday, 1989.

Gibb, Jack. "Climate for Trust Formation." In L. Bradford, Jack Gibb, and K. Benne (eds.), *T-Group Theory and the Laboratory Method.* New York: John Wiley and Sons, 1964.

———. "Dynamics of Leadership and Communication." In E. Pfeiffer (ed.), *Leadership and Social Change.* Iowa City: University Associates Press, 1971, pp. 85–105.

———. "The TORI System of Leadership." In J. Pfeiffer and J. Jones (eds.), *The 1972 Annual Handbook for Group Facilitators.* Iowa City: University Associates Press, 1972.

Goodlad, John. *A Place Named School.* New York: McGraw-Hill, 1983.

Gottfredson, G. D. "A Theory-Ridden Approach to Program Evaluation." *American Psychologist,* Vol. 39 (1984), pp. 1101–1112.

Gouldner, Alvin W. "Cosmopolitans and Locals: Toward an Analysis of Latent Social Roles." *Administrative Science Quarterly,* No. 2 (December 1957), pp. 281–306.

Greenacre, P. "Certain Technical Problems in the Transference Relationship." *Journal of the American Psychoanalytic Association,* Vol. 7 (1959), pp. 484–502.

Haley, J. *Problem-Solving Therapy.* San Francisco, Calif.: Jossey-Bass Publishers, 1976.

Hartmann, Heinz. *Essays in Ego Psychology.* New York: International Universities Press, 1964.

———. *Psychology and the Problem of Adaption.* New York: International Universities Press, 1958.

Hartmann, H., and R. M. Lowenstein. "Notes on the Superego." In *The Psychoanalytic Study of the Child.* New York: International Universities Press, 1962, pp. 42–81.

Herzberg, F. *Work and the Nature of Man.* Cleveland: World Book, 1966.

Hess, Alfred G., Jr. *School Restructuring, Chicago Style.* Newbury Park, Calif.: Corwin Press, 1991.

Hesselbein, F., M. Goldsmith, and R. Beckhard. *The Leader of the Future: New Visions, Strategies, and Practices for the Next Era.* San Francisco: Pfeiffer, 1996.

House, R. J. "A Path Goal Theory of Leadership Effectiveness." *Administrative Science Quarterly* (September 1971), pp. 321–338.

Irvine, Jacqueline Jordan. "Teacher Perspectives: Why Do African-American, Hispanic, and Vietnamese Students Fail?" In Stanley W. Rothstein (ed.), *Handbook of Schooling in Urban America*. Westport, Conn.: Greenwood Press, 1993.

Jacobson, E. *The Self and the Object World*. New York: International Universities Press, 1964.

Johnson, D. *Reaching Out: Interpersonal Effectiveness and Self-Actualization*. Englewood Cliffs, N.J.: Prentice-Hall, 1981.

Johnson, D., and F. Johnson. *Joining Together*. Englewood Cliffs, N.J.: Prentice-Hall, 1982.

Johnson, D., and M. Noonan. "The Effects of Acceptance and Reciprocation of Self-Disclosures on the Development of Trust." *Journal of Counseling Psychology*, No. 19 (1972), pp. 411–416.

Jones, E. E., J. D. Cumming, and M. J. Horowitz. "Another Look at the Nonspecific Hypothesis of Therapeutic Effectiveness." *Journal of Consulting and Clinical Psychology*, Vol. 56 (1988), pp. 40–47.

Joyce, B., R. Hersh, and M. McKibbin. *The Structure of School Improvement*. New York: Longman, 1983.

Kanfer, F. H., and B. K. Schefft. *Guiding Therapeutic Change*. Champaign, Ill.: Research Press, 1988.

Kanfer, F. H., and A. P. Goldstein (eds.). *Helping People Change: A Textbook of Methods*. New York: Pergamon Press, 1986.

Karp, H. B. *The Change Leader: Using a Gestalt Approach with Work Groups*. San Francisco: Pfeiffer, 1996.

Katz, Daniel, and Robert L. Kahn. *The Social Psychology of Organizations*. 2nd ed. New York: John Wiley and Sons, 1978.

Katznelson, I., and M. Weir. *Schooling for All: Class, Race, and the Decline of the Democratic Ideal*. New York: Basic Books, 1985.

Kimble, G. A. "Psychology's Two Cultures." *American Psychologist*, Vol. 39 (1984), pp. 833–839.

Kinlaw, D. C. *Coaching for Commitment: Managerial Strategies for Obtaining Superior Performance*. San Francisco: Pfeiffer, 1996.

———. *Listening and Communicating Skills*. San Diego: University Associates Press, 1982.

Knapp, M. L. *Nonverbal Communication in Human Interaction*. New York: Holt, Rinehart and Winston, 1978.

Kozol, Jonathan. *Savage Inequalities: Children in America's Schools*. New York: Harper, 1991.

Kris, E. "The Recovery of Childhood Memories in Psychoanalysis." In *The Psychoanalytic Study of the Child*. New York: International Universities Press, 1956, pp. 54–58.

Lacan, J. "The Function of Language in Psychoanalysis." In W. E. Steinkraus (ed.), *The Language of the Self*. Baltimore: John Hopkins University Press, 1968.

———. *The Seminar of Jacques Lacan*, Book II. Jacques-Alain Miller (ed.), Sylvana Tomaselli (trans.). New York: W. W. Norton, 1991.

———. *Speech and Language in Psychoanalysis*. Anthony Wilden (trans.). Baltimore: Johns Hopkins University Press, 1989.

Lassey, William. "Dimensions of Leadership." In William Lassey (ed.), *Leadership and Social Change.* Iowa City: University Associates Press, 1971.

Likert, R. *The Human Organization, Its Management and Value.* New York: McGraw-Hill, 1967.

Lutz, F., and C. Mertz. *The Politics of School/Community Relations.* New York: Teachers College Press, 1992.

Mackenzie, Gordon N., and Stephen M. Corey. *Instructional Leadership.* New York: Teachers College Press, 1954.

Mahler, M. S. *On Human Symbiosis and the Vicissitudes of Individuation.* New York: International Universities Press, 1968.

Mahoney, M. J., and D. B. Arnkoff. "Cognitive and Self-Control Therapies." In S. L. Garfield and A. E. Bergin, (eds.), *Handbook of Psychotherapy and Behavior Change.* New York: Wiley, 1978.

Mannheim, K., and W. A. C. Stewart. *An Introduction to the Sociology of Education.* London: Routledge & Kegan Paul, 1962.

Marshall, Ray, and Marc Tucker. *Thinking for a Living: Education and the Wealth of Nations.* York: Basic Books, 1992.

Maurer, R. *Beyond the Wall of Resistance: Unconventional Strategies That Build Support for Change.* San Francisco: Pfeiffer, 1996.

Meyer, Marshal W. et al. *Environments and Organizations.* San Francisco: Jossey-Bass, 1978.

Miller, L. M. *American Spirit: Visions of a New Corporate Culture.* New York: Morrow, 1984.

Murphy, J. J. *Pulling Together: The Power of Teamwork.* San Francisco: Pfeiffer, 1996.

Nasaw, David. *Schooled to Order: A Social History of Public Schooling in the United States.* New York: Oxford University Press, 1979.

Neimeyer, G. J., and P. G. Banikiotes. "Self-Disclosure Flexibility, Empathy, and Perceptions of Adjustment and Attraction." *Journal of Counseling Psychology,* Vol. 28 (1981), pp. 272–275.

Ogbu, John. *Minority Education and Caste.* New York: Academic Press, 1978.

Owens, Robert G. *Organizational Behavior in Education.* Boston: Allyn & Bacon, 1995.

Pyszczynski, T., and J. Greenberg. "Self-Regulatory Perseveration and Its Depressive Self-Focusing Style: A Self-Awareness Theory of Depression." *Psychological Bulletin,* Vol. 102 (1987), pp. 122–138.

Rappaport, J. "In Praise of Paradox: A Social Policy of Empowerment over Prevention." *American Journal of Community Psychology,* Vol. 9 (1981), pp. 1–26.

Redl, F., and D. Wineman. *The Aggressive Child.* Glencoe, Ill.: Free Press, 1957.

———. *Children Who Hate.* New York: Free Press, 1951.

———. *Controls from Within.* New York: Free Press, 1952.

Robertshaw, J. E., and M. N. Rerick. *Problem-Solving: A Systems Approach.* New York: Petrocelli Books, 1978.

Robinson, M. D. *Meaningful Counseling.* New York: Human Sciences Press, 1988.

Rogers, C. R. "Reflections on Feelings." *Person Centered Review,* No. 2 (1986), pp. 375–377.

Rothstein, Stanley W. "Building and Maintaining High Trust Climates: Training the New Administrator in Feeling Expression and Inquiry Skills." *Education and Urban Society* (November 1976), pp. 81–101.

———. "Conflict Resolution in a Supportive Environment." *Education and Urban Society*, Vol. VII, No. 2 (February 1975), pp. 193–206.

———. "The Ethics of Coercion." *Urban Education*, Vol. XXII, No. 1 (April 1987), pp. 53–72.

———. "The First Supportive Environment." *The Clearing House*, Vol. 50, No. 8 (April 1977), pp. 357–360.

———. "The Focus Interview." *The Guidance Clinic* (December 1981), pp. 1–15.

———. *Identity and Ideology: Socio-Cultural Theories of Schooling*. Westport, Conn.: Greenwood Press, 1991.

———. "Journal of a Ghetto School." *The Crisis*, National Journal of the NAACP (March 1975), pp. 84–86.

———. "The Language of Acceptance in the Supervisory Process." *The Guidance Clinic* (December 1986), pp. 1–14.

———. "Orientations: First Impressions in an Urban Junior High School." *Urban Education*, Vol. 14, No. 1 (April 1979), pp. 91–92.

———. "Researching the Power Structure: Personalized Power and Institutionalized Charisma in the Principalship." *Interchange: Journal of the Ontario Institute for the Study of Education*, Vol. 6, No. 2 (1975), pp. 41–48.

———. *Schooling the Poor: A Social Inquiry into the American Educational Experience*. Westport, Conn.: Bergin & Garvey, 1994.

———. *Schools and Society: New Perspectives in American Education*. Englewood Cliffs, N.J.: Prentice-Hall, 1996.

———. "Supervisory Relationship." *The Guidance Clinic* (January 1987), pp. 1–15.

———. "Supportive Supervision: Leadership for the 21st Century." In Andrew Dubin (ed.), *Leadership for the 21st Century*. London: Falmar Press, 1991.

———. "The Socialization of the School Administrator." *Private School Quarterly* (Spring 1983), pp. 52–60.

———. "Teachers and Students in Urban Schools." In Stanley W. Rothstein (ed.), *Handbook of Schooling in Urban America*. Westport, Conn.: Greenwood Press, 1993.

———. "The Tip of the Iceberg: Teacher Distrust of Administrators." *The Clearing House*, Vol. 53, No. 5 (January 1980), pp. 24–28.

———. *The Voice of the Other: Language as Illusion in the Formation of the Self*. Westport, Conn.: Praeger Publishers, 1993.

Rothwell, W. J., R. Sullivan, and G. N. McLean. *Practicing Organizational Development: A Guide for Consultants*. San Francisco: Pfeiffer, 1996.

Roudinesco, Elisabeth. *Jacques Lacan & Co.: A History of Psychoanalysis in France, 1925–1985*. Chicago: University of Chicago Press, 1986.

Schmuck, Richard A., and Matthew R. Miles (eds.). *Organizational Development in Schools*. Palo Alto, Calif.: National Press Books, 1971.

Schumpteter, Joseph. *Capitalism, Socialism, and Democracy*. New York: Harper & Brothers, 1970.

Schwarz, R. *The Skilled Facilitator: Practical Wisdom for Developing Effective Groups*. San Francisco: Pfeiffer, 1996.

Sergiovanni, Thomas J., and Robert J. Starratt. *Supervision: Human Perspectives*. New York: McGraw-Hill, 1988.

Shakeshaft, Charol. "Meeting the Needs of Girls in Urban Schools." In Stanley W.

Rothstein (ed.), *Handbook of Schooling in Urban America*. Westport, Conn.: Greenwood Press, pp. 175–188.

Simmel, Georg. *Conflict and the Web of Group Affiliations*. Glencoe, Ill.: Free Press, 1955.

———. *The Sociology of Georg Simmel*. K. Wolff (trans.). Glencoe, Ill.: Free Press, 1950.

Spitz, R. A. *The First Year of Life*. New York: International Press, 1965.

Stepsis, J. A. "Structure as an Integrative Concept in Management: Theory and Practice." In John E. Jones and J. William, Pfeiffer (eds.), *The 1977 Annual Handbook for Group Facilitators*. La Jolla, Calif.: University Associates Press, pp. 169–179.

Surra, C, and R. Milardo. "The Social Psychological Context of Developing Relationships." In W. H. Jones and D. Perlman (eds.), *Advances in Personal Relationships*, Vol. 3. London: Jessica Kingsley, 1991.

Thomas, William G. "Experiential Education—A Rationale for Creative Problem Solving." *Education and Urban Society* (February 1975), pp. 172–181.

Tonnies, F. *Community and Society*. C. P. Loomis (trans.). East Lansing, Mich.: Michigan State University, 1957.

Tweedle, Patricia G. "Crack Kids: An Emerging Education Dilemma." In Stanley W. Rothstein (ed.), *Handbook of Schooling in Urban America*. Westport, Conn.: Greenwood Press, 1993, pp. 271–286.

Waller, Willard. *The Sociology of Teaching*. New York: Russell & Russell, 1961.

———. "What Teaching Does to Teachers." In M. Stein, A. Vidich, and S. White (eds.), *Identity and Anxiety*. Glencoe, Ill.: Free Press, 1962.

Walsh, F. "Conceptualization of Normal Family Processes." In F. Walsh (ed.), *Normal Family Processes*. New York: Guilford, 1993.

Warwick, David. "Ideologies, Integration and Conflicts of Meaning." In M. Flude and J. Ahier (eds.), *Educability, Schools and Ideology*. London: Croom Helm, 1974.

Weber, Max. *The Theory of Social and Economic Organization*. New York: Free Press, 1966.

Weeres, Joseph G. "The Organizational Structures of Urban Educational Systems: Bureaucratic Practices in Mass Societies." In S. W. Rothstein (ed.), *Handbook of Schooling in Urban America*. Westport, Conn.: Greenwood Press, 1993, pp. 113–130.

Wiley, G. E. "Win/Lose Situations." In J. Jones and W. Pfeiffer (eds.), *The 1973 Annual Handbook for Group Facilitators*. San Diego: University Associates, 1973.

Wilson, John. "Power, Paranoia, and Education." *Interchange: A Quarterly Review of Education*, Vol. XXII, No. 33 (1994), pp. 43-54.

Wood, Julia T. *Relational Communication*. Belmont, Calif.: Wadsworth Publishing Company, 1995.

Wynn, R., and C. Guditus. *Team Management: Leadership by Consensus*. Columbus, Ohio: Charles E. Merrill Publishing Company, 1984.

Yukl, Gary A. *Leadership in Organizations*. Englewood Cliffs, N.J.: Prentice-Hall, 1989.

Index

About the Authors

RAYMOND C. GARUBO is Professor of Public Administration at the University of La Verne, California.

STANLEY WILLIAM ROTHSTEIN is Professor of Administration and Social Foundations at California State University, Fullerton.